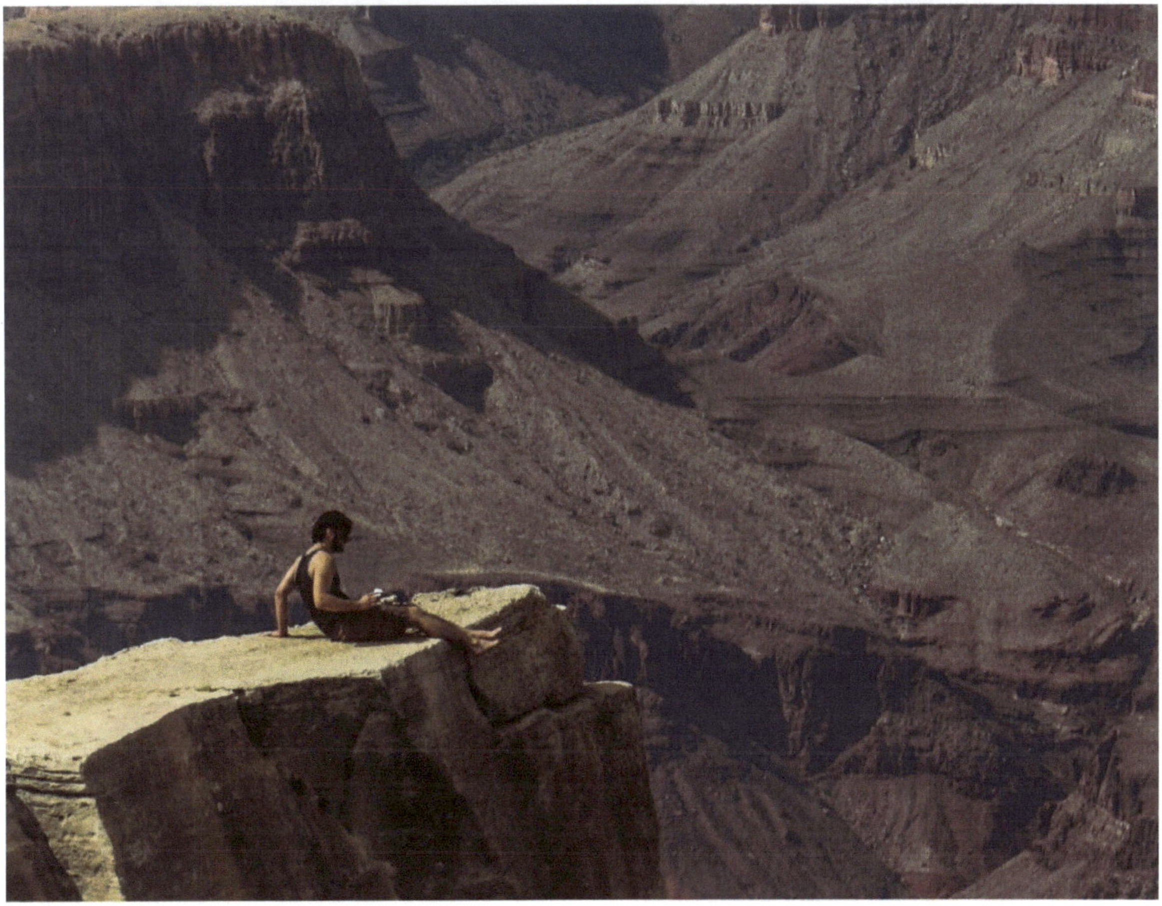

A Guide to the Grand Canyon's South Rim
by Kathleen Odenthal Romano

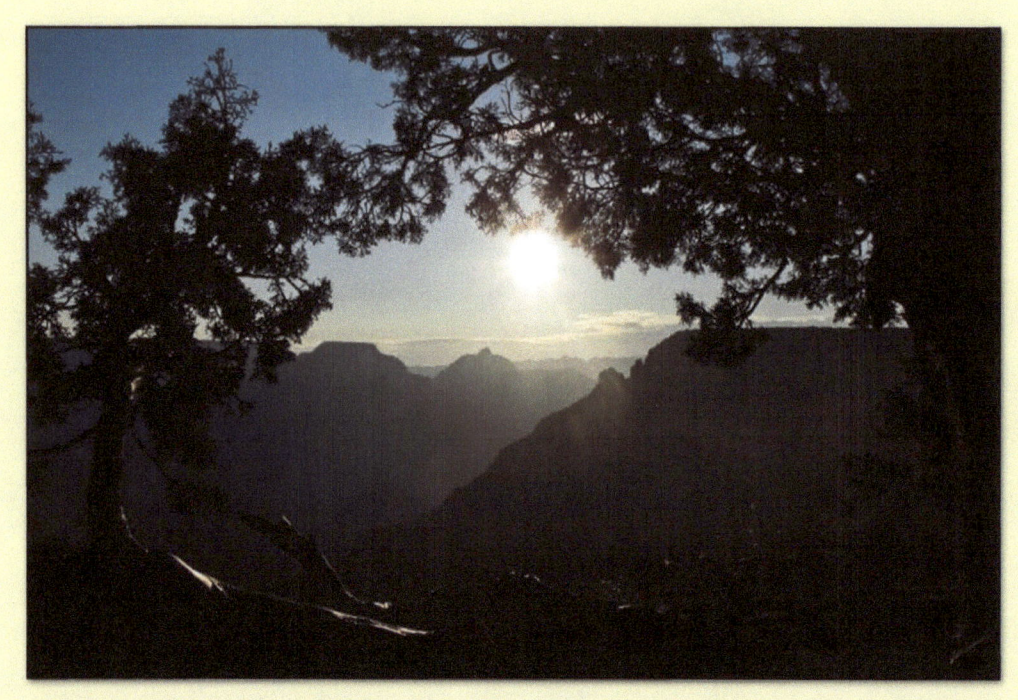

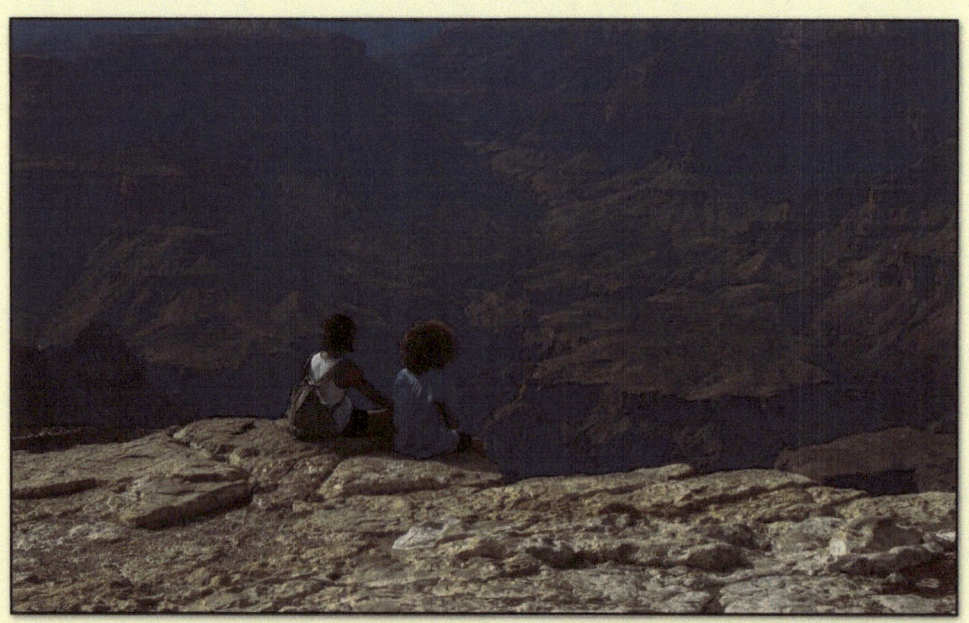

Grand Canyon National Park

The Grand Canyon, one of the seven world wonders, is on almost every explorer's bucket list.

President Theodore Roosevelt called the Grand Canyon "the one great sight which every American should see."

The canyon is 277 miles wide, 18 miles long and attains a depth of up to 1 mile in certain locations. The Colorado River runs through the canyon. This majestic sight is part of the Grand Canyon National Park, a World Heritage Sight since 1973.

From helicopter rides through the peaks of the canyons to canoe trips up the Colorado River, there is so much to do, and even more to take in when you go to the Grand Canyon.

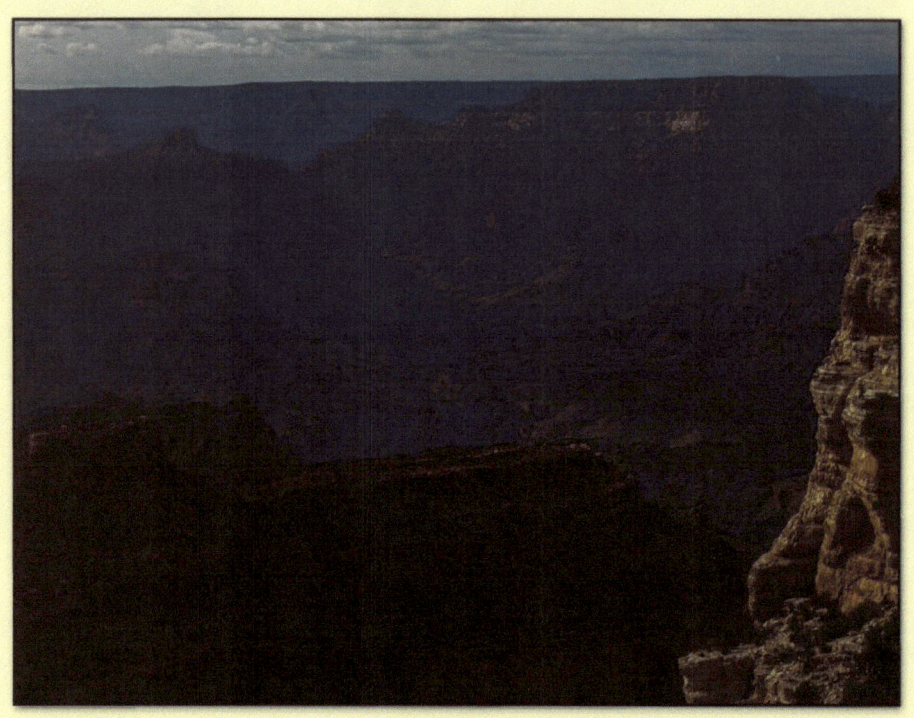

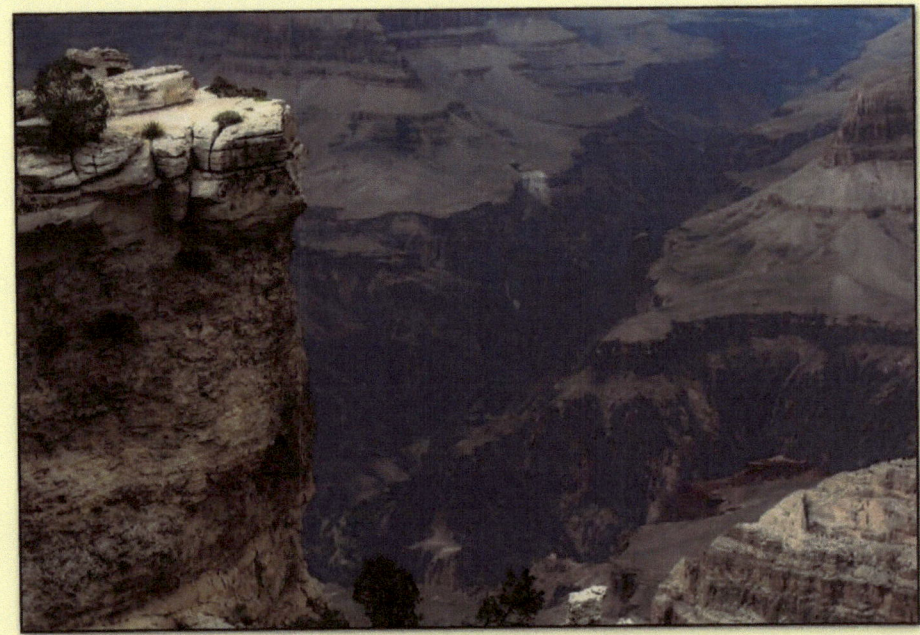

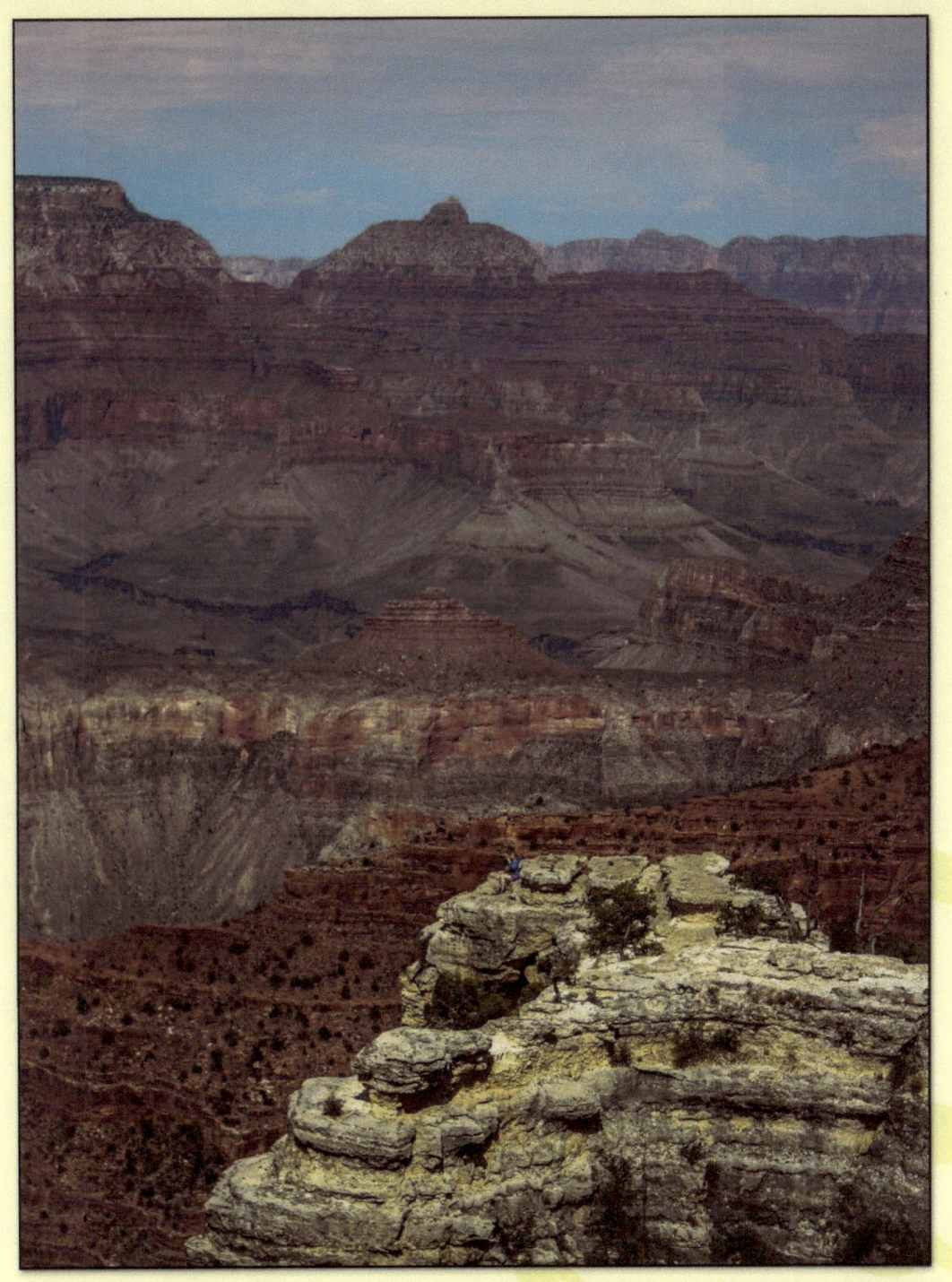

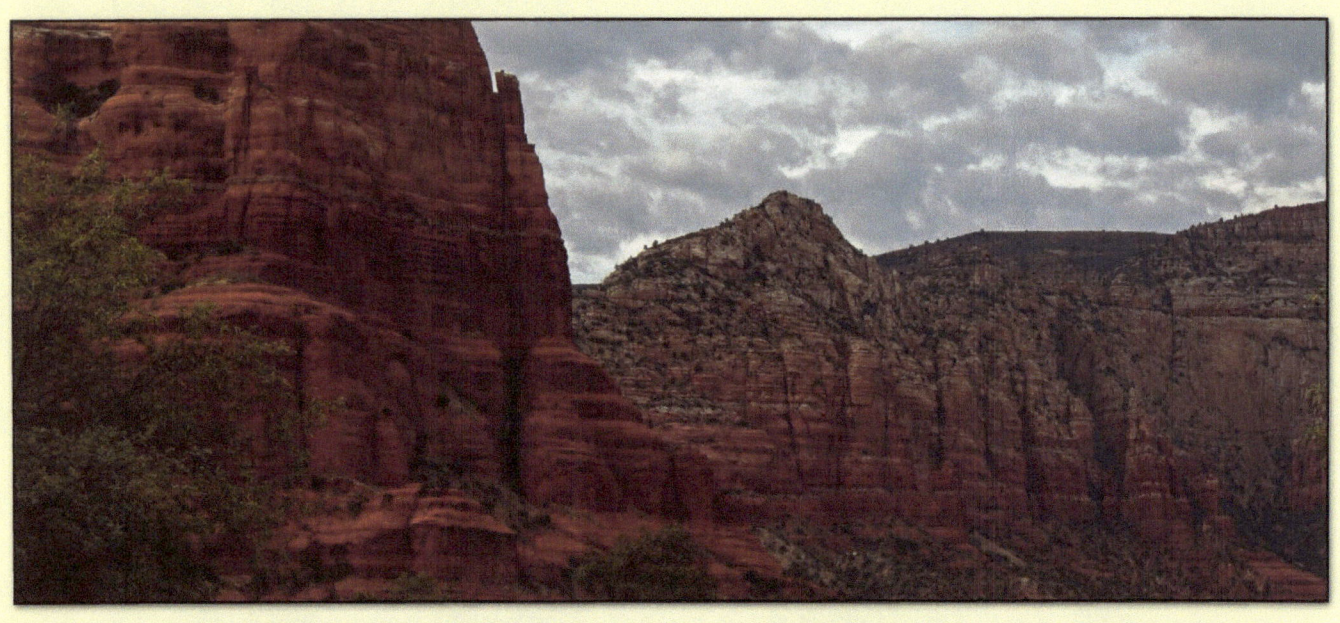

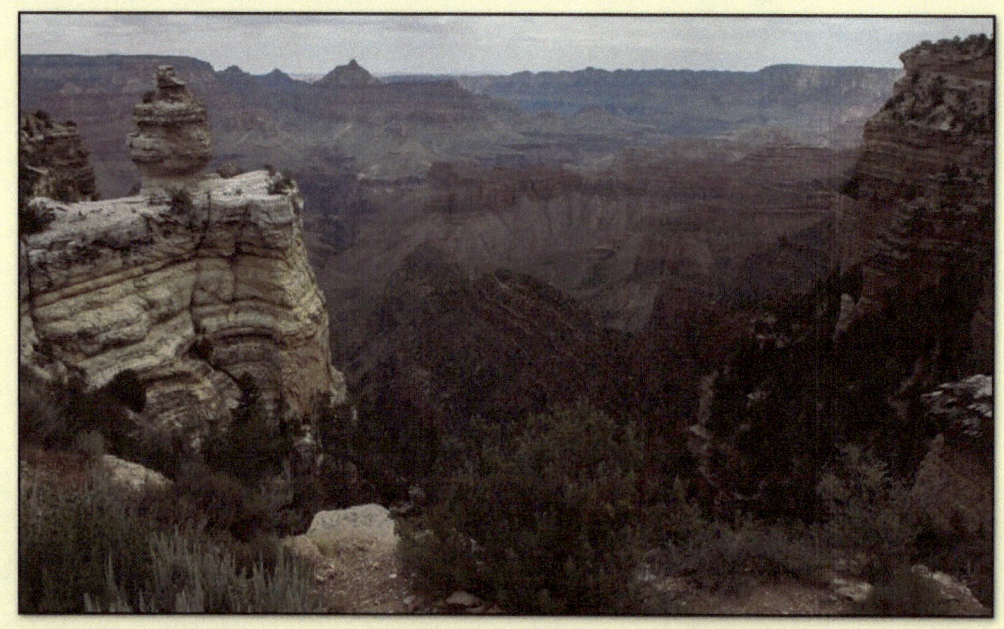

The Grand Canyon is the one place where you can see the evolution of the planet's landscape dating back tens of millions of years visibly through nature.

Carved by the water flowing down the Colorado River, the Grand Canyon is managed by the Navajo people, the Hualapai Tribal Nation and the Havasupai Tribe. Every year the canyon evolves due to surging water and eroding rock formations.

The canyon is 18 miles wide at the furthest point between the rims, and four miles wide at the narrowest points. The length of the canyon spans over 100 miles. Depending on where you are located, the canyon can reach as high as 9,000 feet in elevation.

The Grand Canyon is a popular place for photographers, hikers, and anyone with an appreciation for nature. There is plenty to do, plenty to see and plenty of reasons to visit!

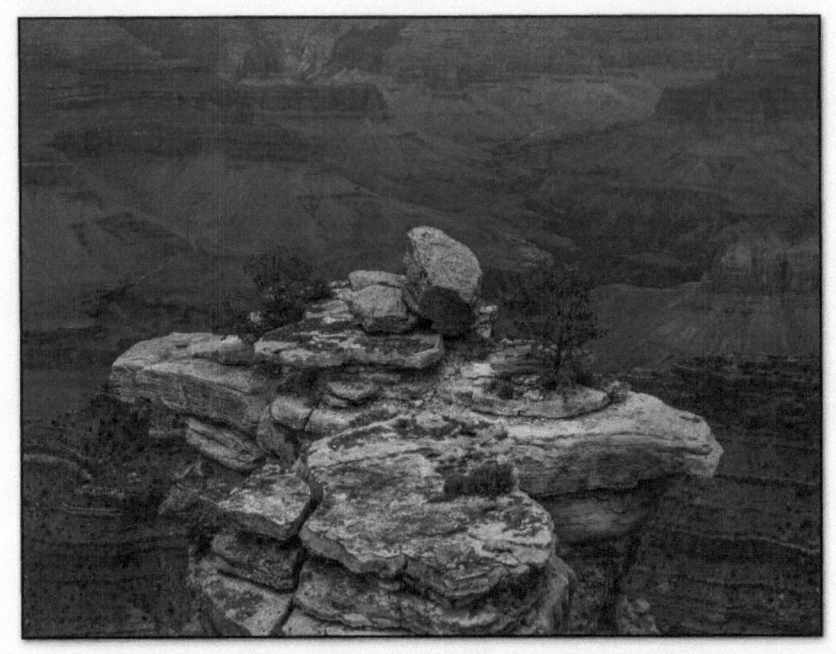

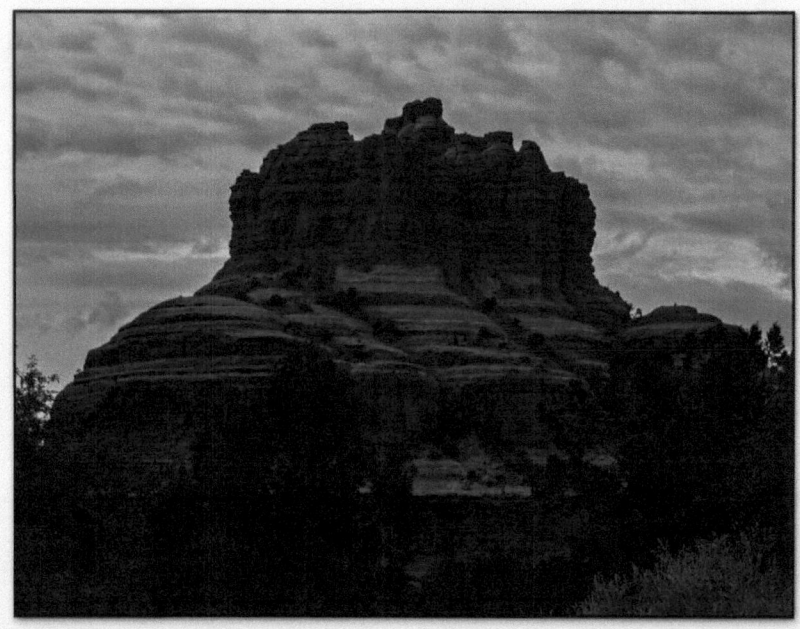

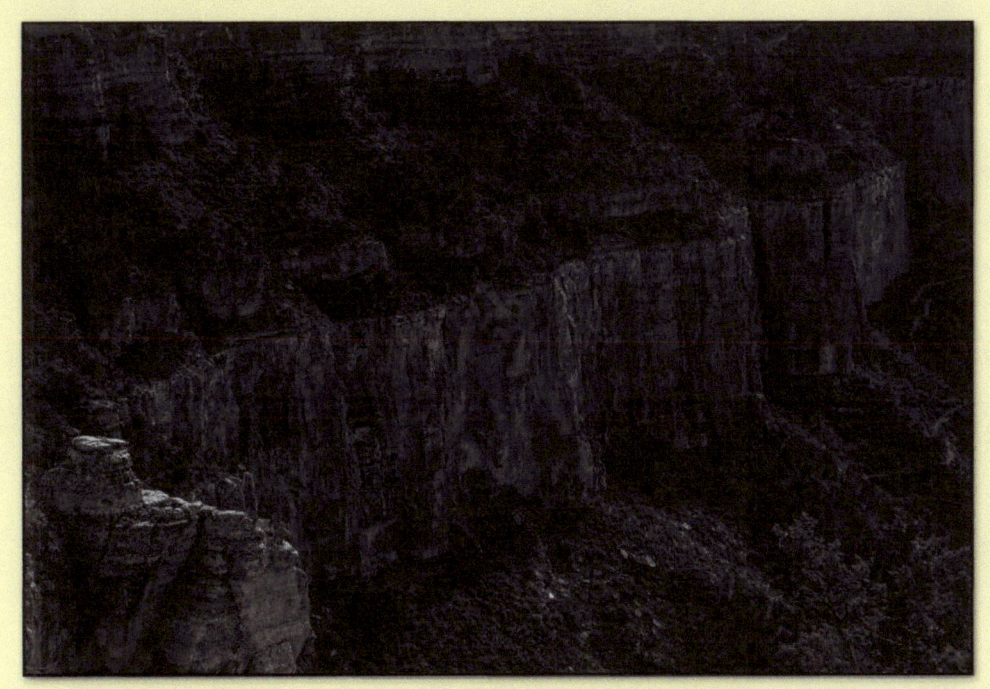

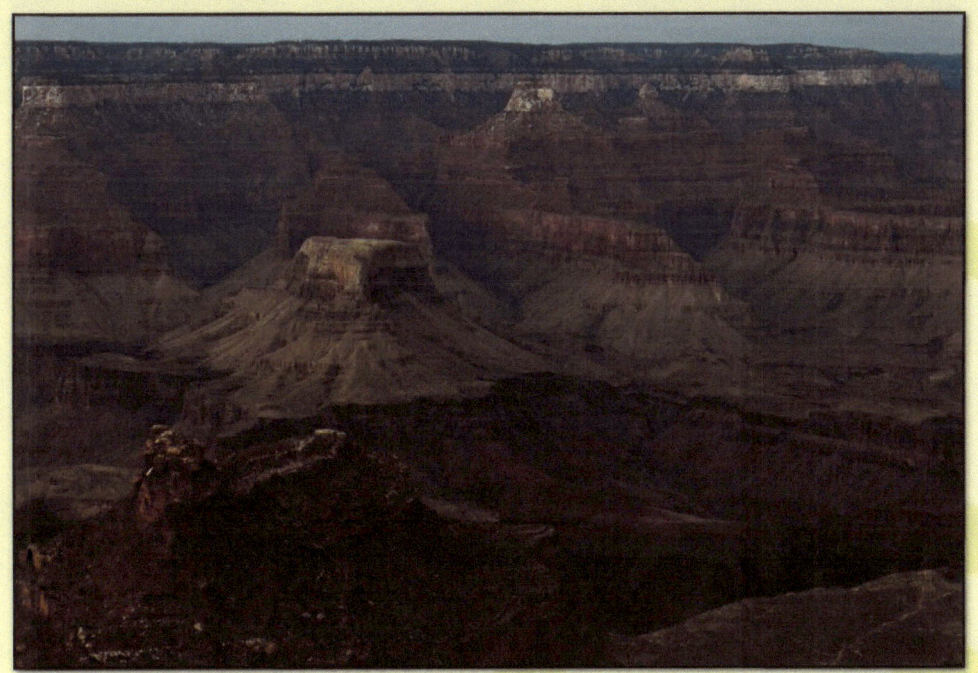

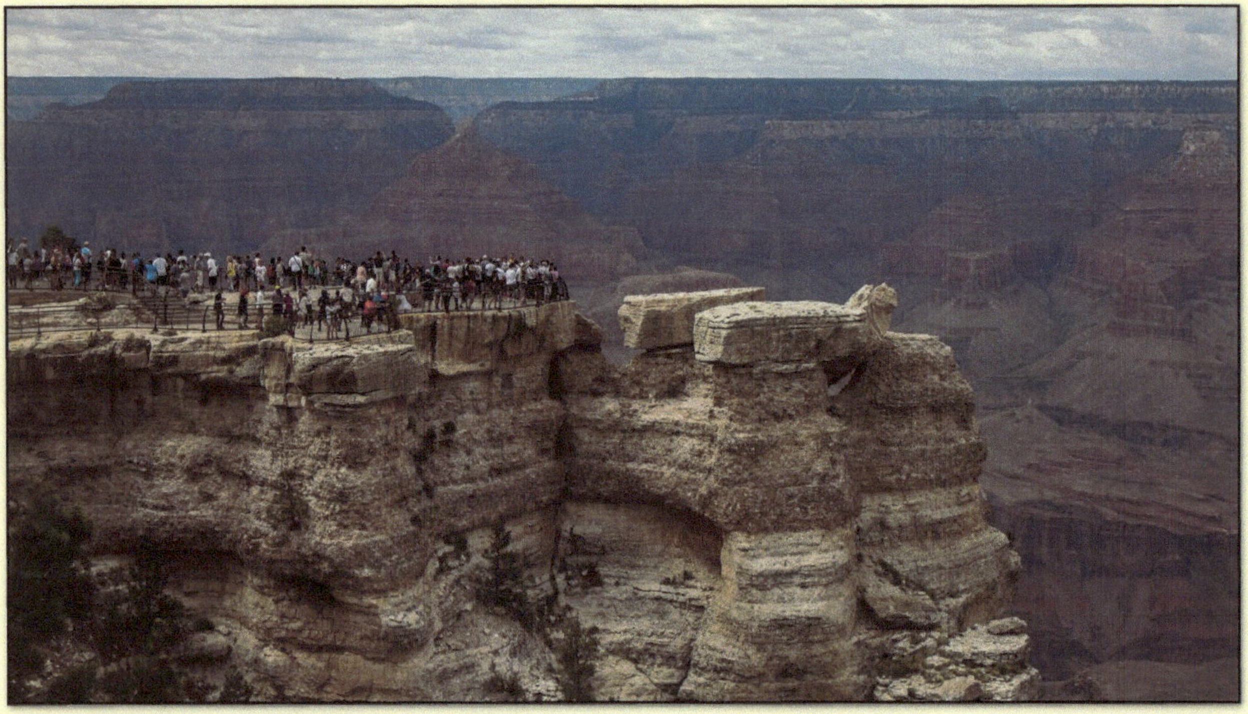

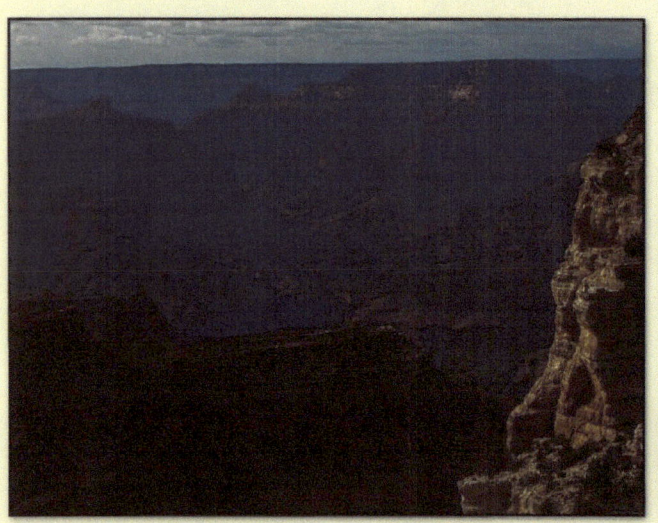
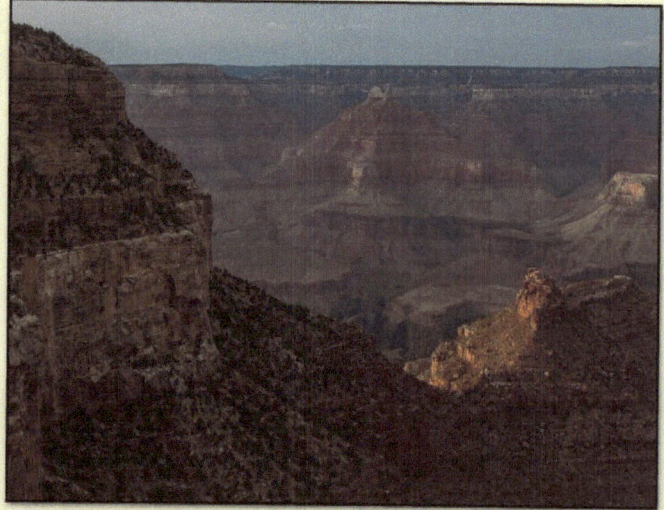

Grand Canyon's North Rim Compared to the South Rim

The south rim of the canyon is much more popular than the north rim. This isn't due to a lack of scenery at the canyon's north rim, but because it is more remote and consists of more rugged terrain.

Ideal for serious hikers and those looking to escape the many tourists at the south rim, the Grand Canyon's north rim is 1,000 feet higher in elevation and provides completely different views than the south rim.

Three of the canyon's top overlooks are located at the Grand Canyon's north rim. These include Tuweep, Point Sublime and Cape Royal. Although higher in elevation, views of the Colorado River are supposedly best from the north rim.

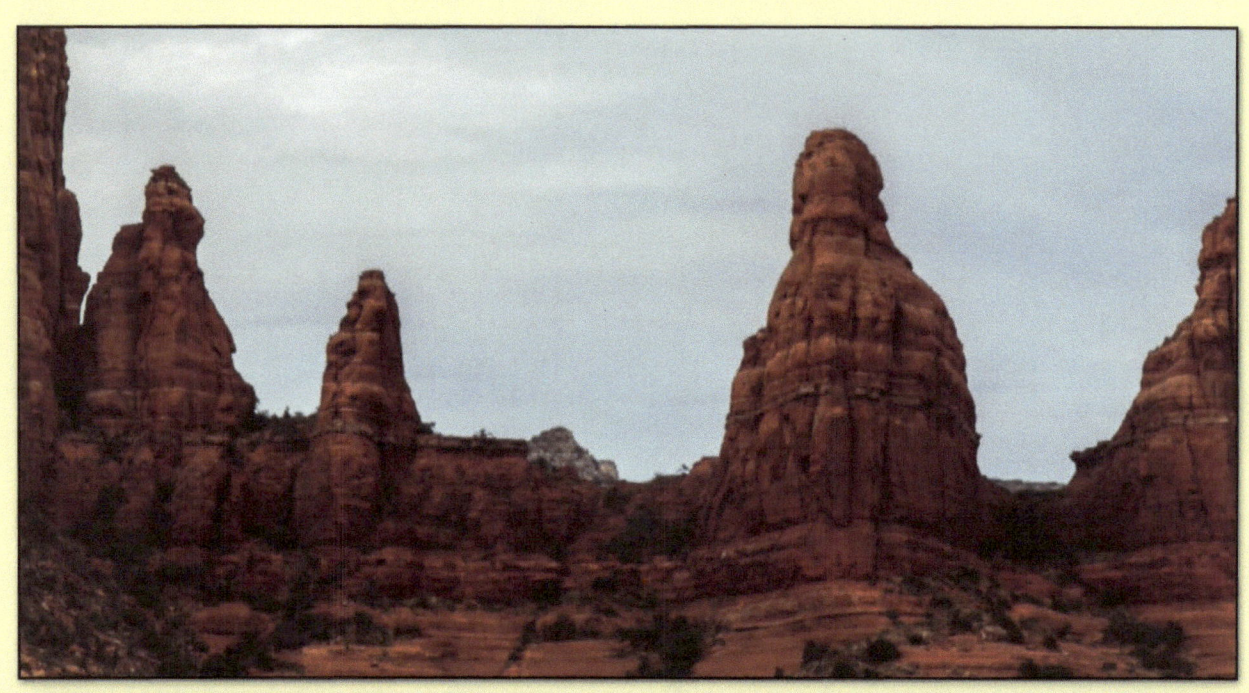

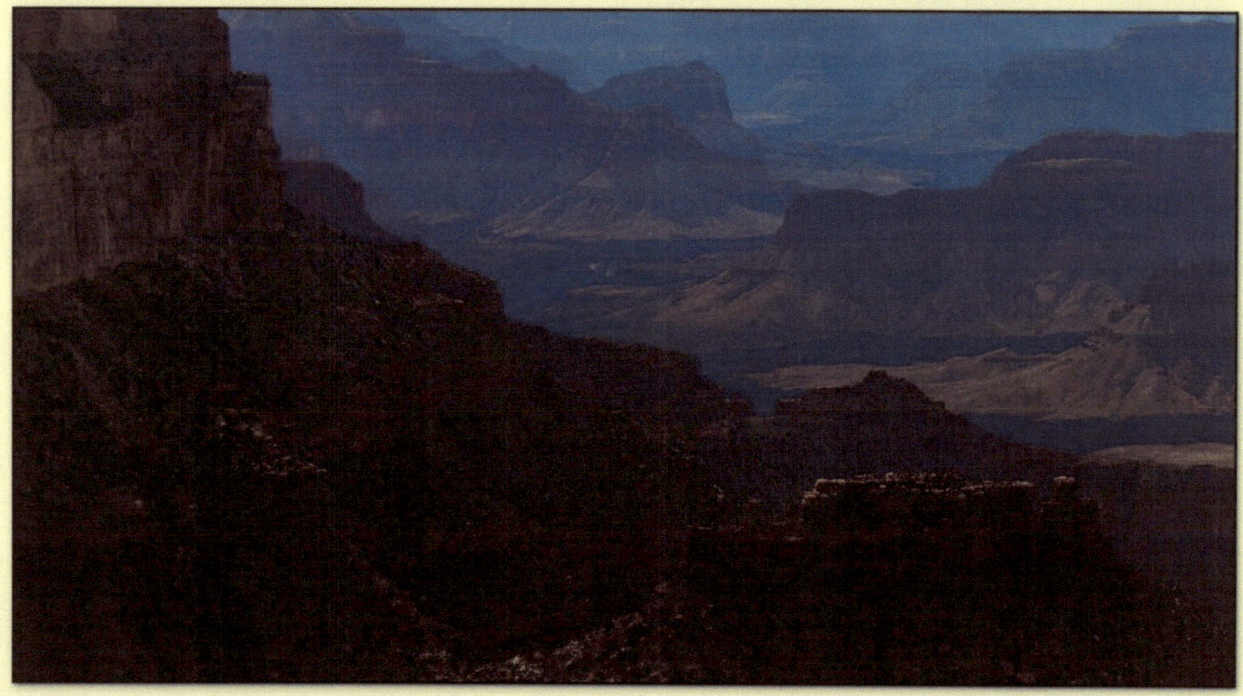

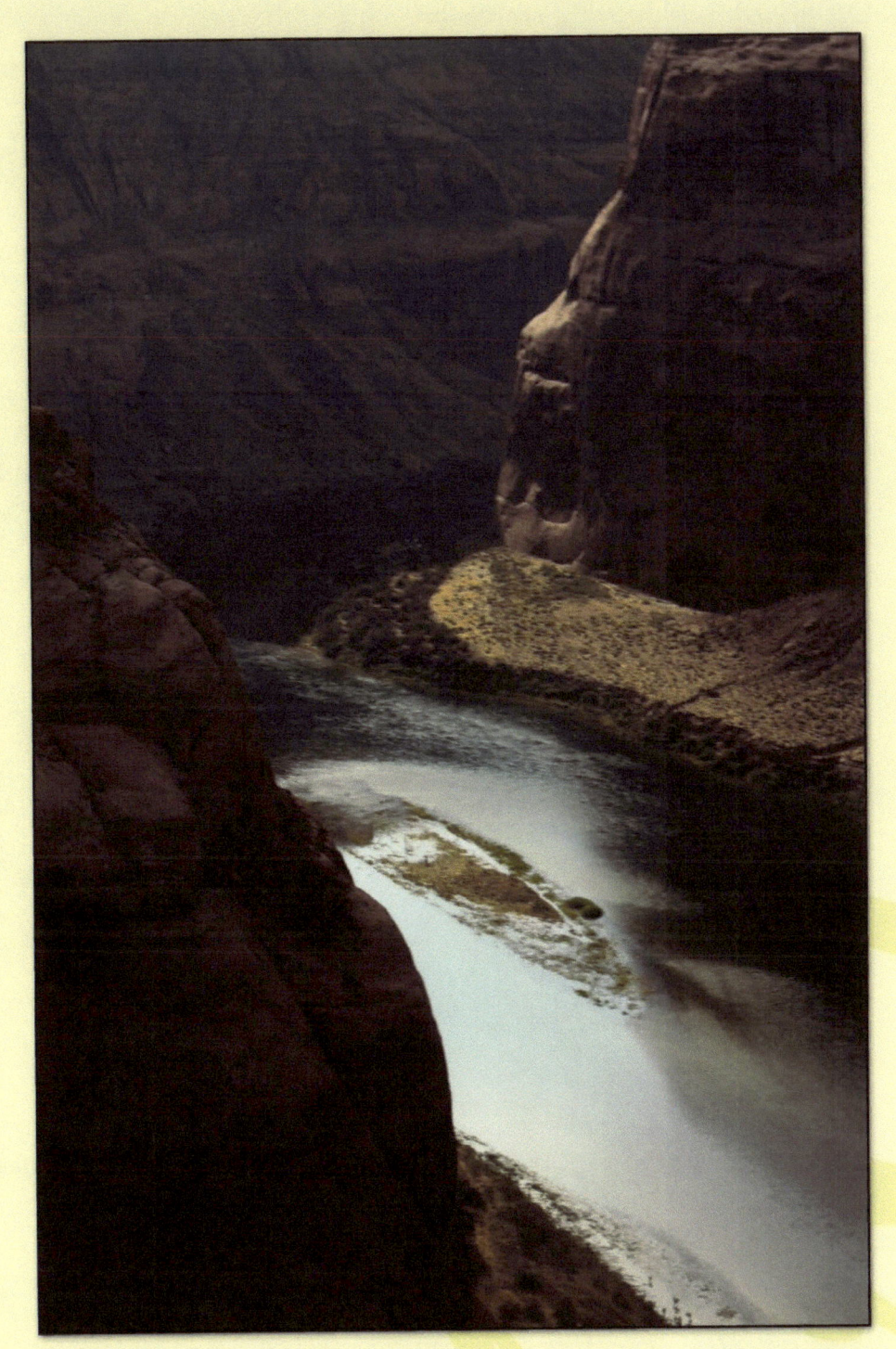

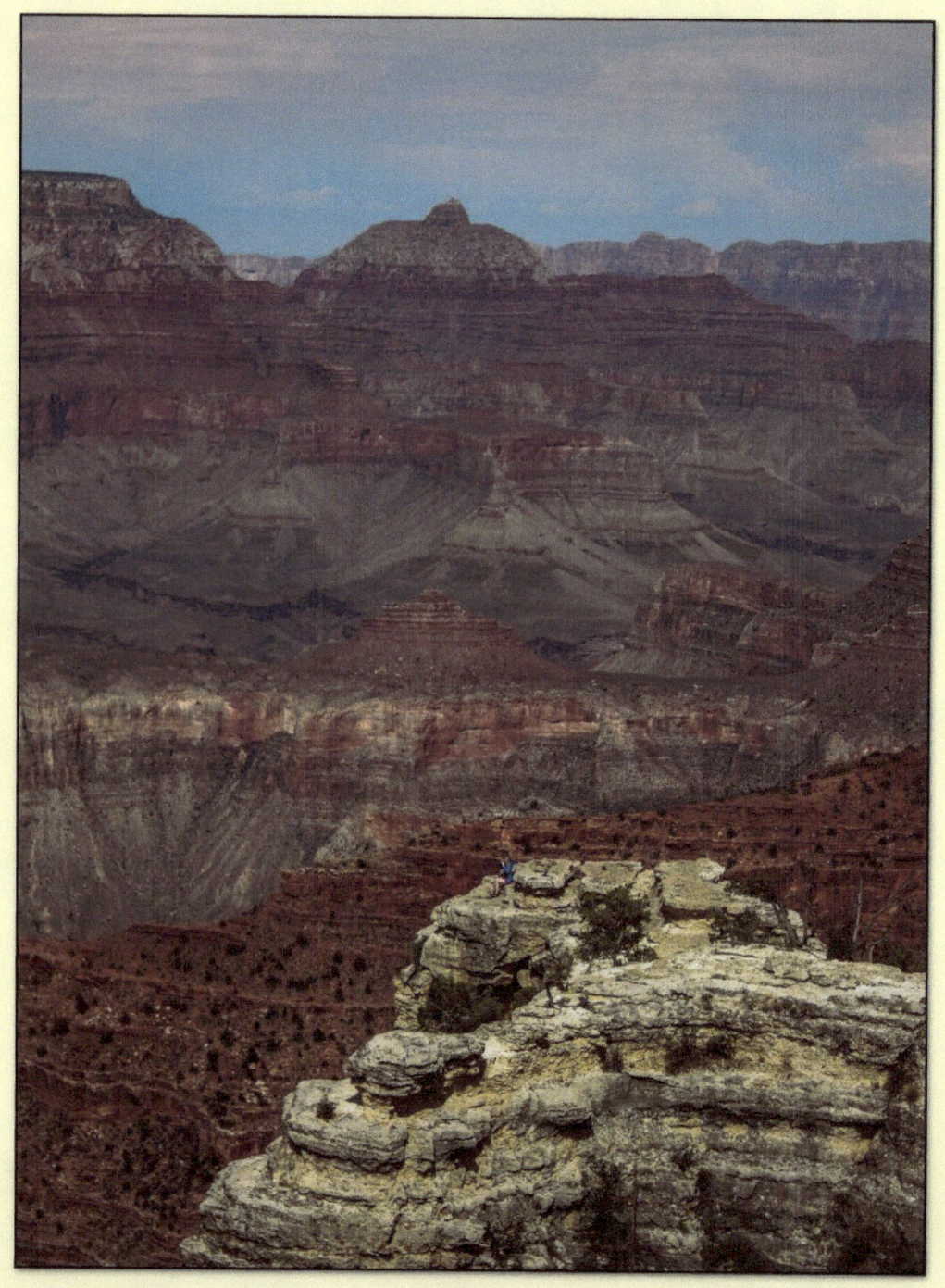

Trails to Hike at the Grand Canyon's South Rim

The Rim Trail- Extending from Grand Canyon Village to the Hermits Rest overlook, this trail is a good day trail for the novice hiker. Although the trail technically stretches for miles along the south rim, several free buses drive throughout the park to shuttle people from point to point, making it easy to cater your hike to your needs.

Bright Angel Trail- This popular trail of the south rim starts just west of Bright Angel Lodge and consists of twelve miles round trip. Although the trail does feature some shady parts, it is quite steep and only recommended for those who have experience hiking.

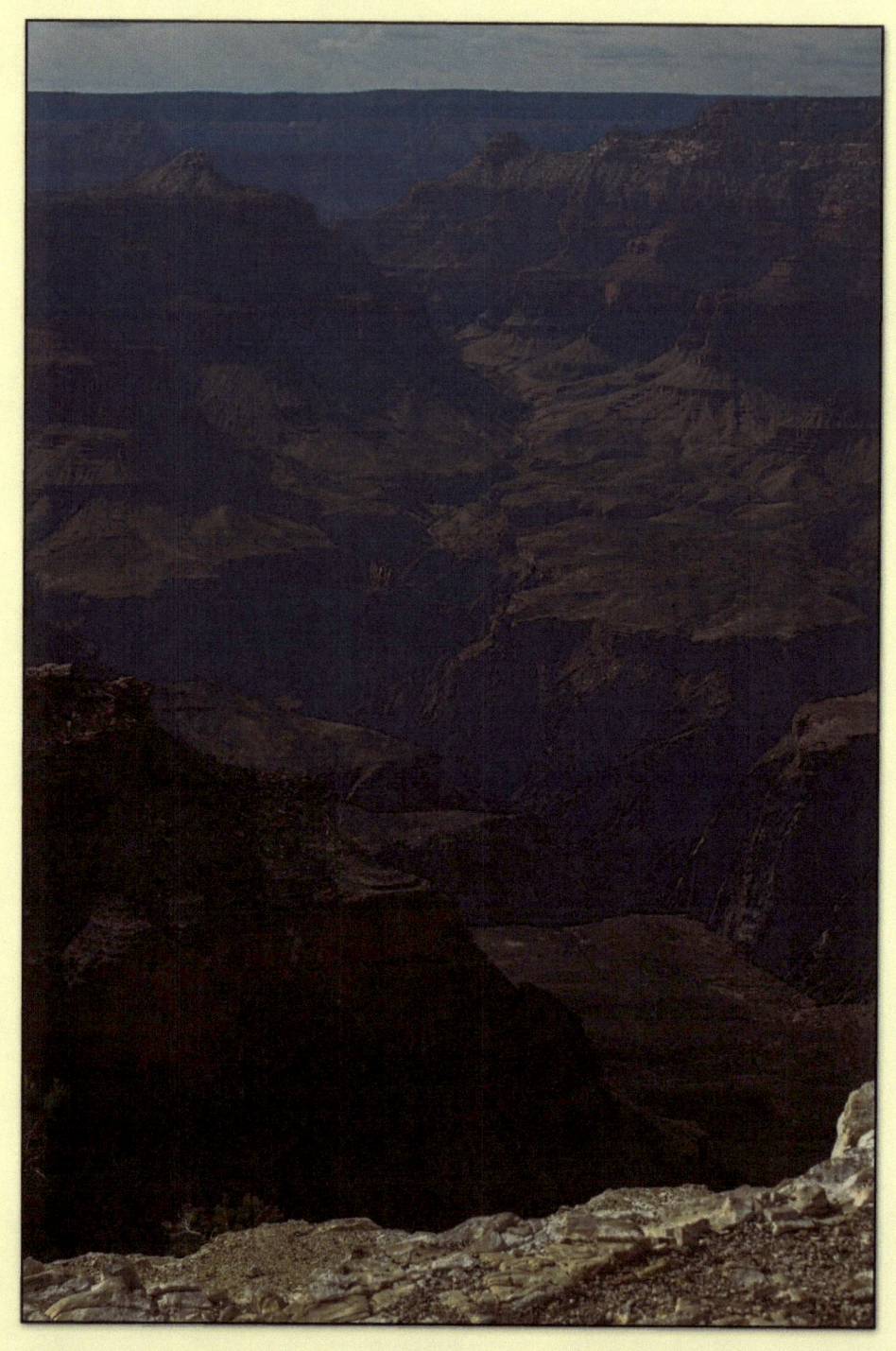

Trails to Hike at the Grand Canyon's South Rim

The Rim Trail- Extending from Grand Canyon Village to the Hermits Rest overlook, this trail is a good day trail for the novice hiker. Although the trail technically stretches for miles along the south rim, several free buses drive throughout the park to shuttle people from point to point, making it easy to cater your hike to your needs.

Bright Angel Trail- This popular trail of the south rim starts just west of Bright Angel Lodge and consists of twelve miles round trip. Although the trail does feature some shady parts, it is quite steep and only recommended for those who have experience hiking.

South Kaibab Trail- The start of this challenging trail begins near Yaki Point. Although the hike is only six miles round trip, the hike is fairly steep and no water is available along the way. If you happen to be in good shape and have hiking experience, this trail offers some of the best vistas available on the south rim.

The Hike from Phantom Ranch- One of the most challenging, yet rewarding hikes is the hike from Phantom Ranch to the top of the canyon. Phantom Ranch is a small cabin located at the bottom of the canyon, right off of the Colorado River. Hikers sleep at the cabin overnight, and typically hit the trail before 5 a.m. to avoid heat exhaustion. The hike can take an entire day for even expert hikers, and is not recommended for those with minimal hiking experience, as well as people with health conditions.

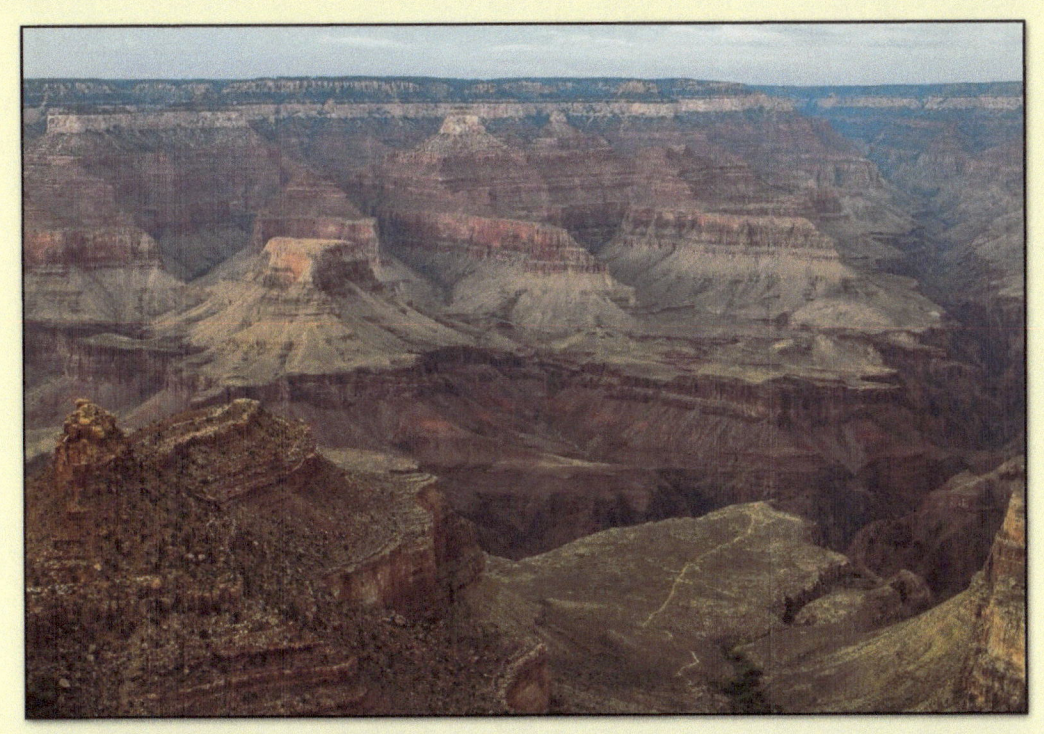

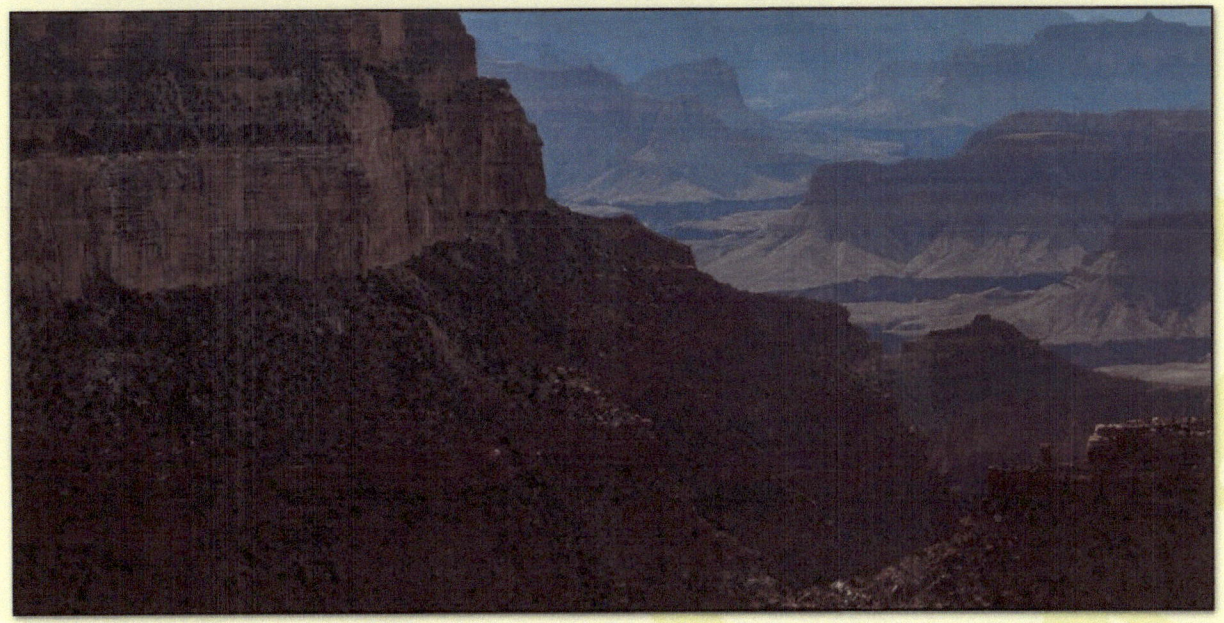

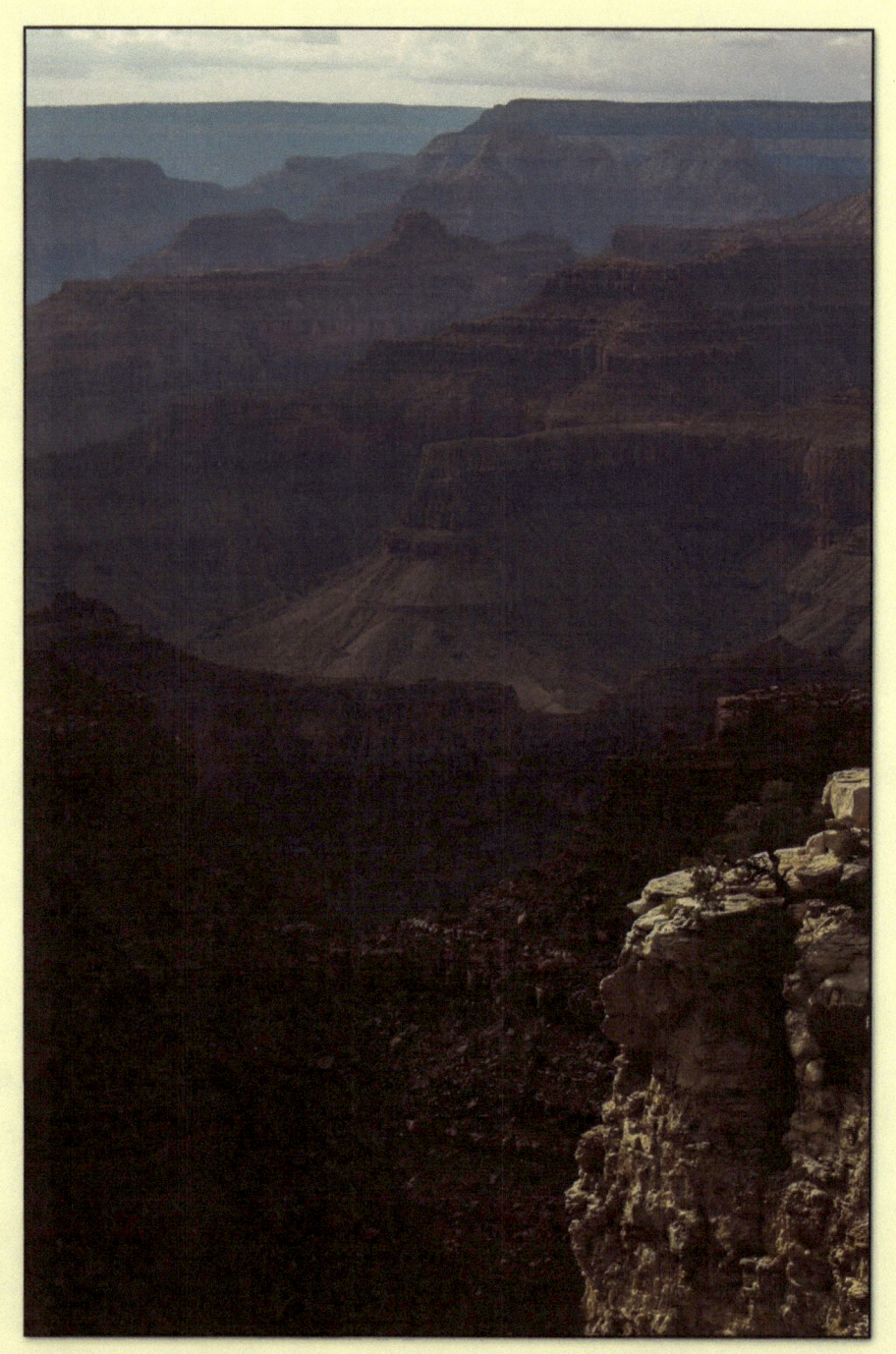

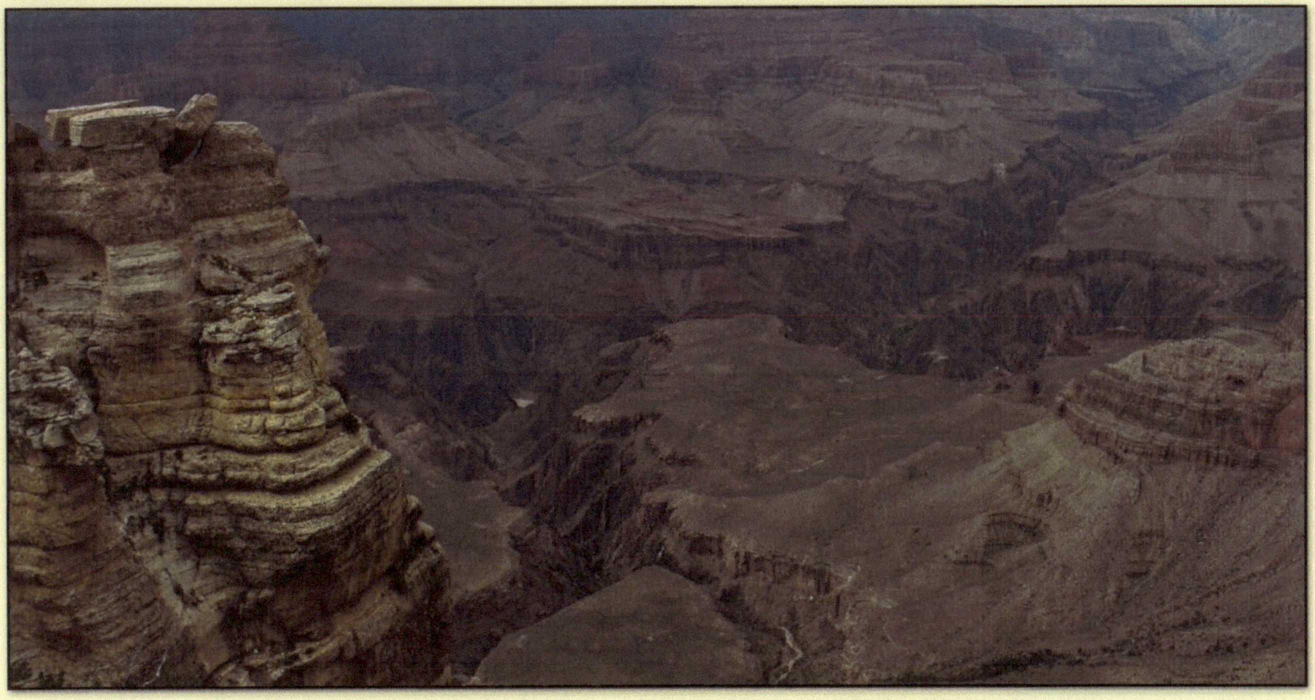

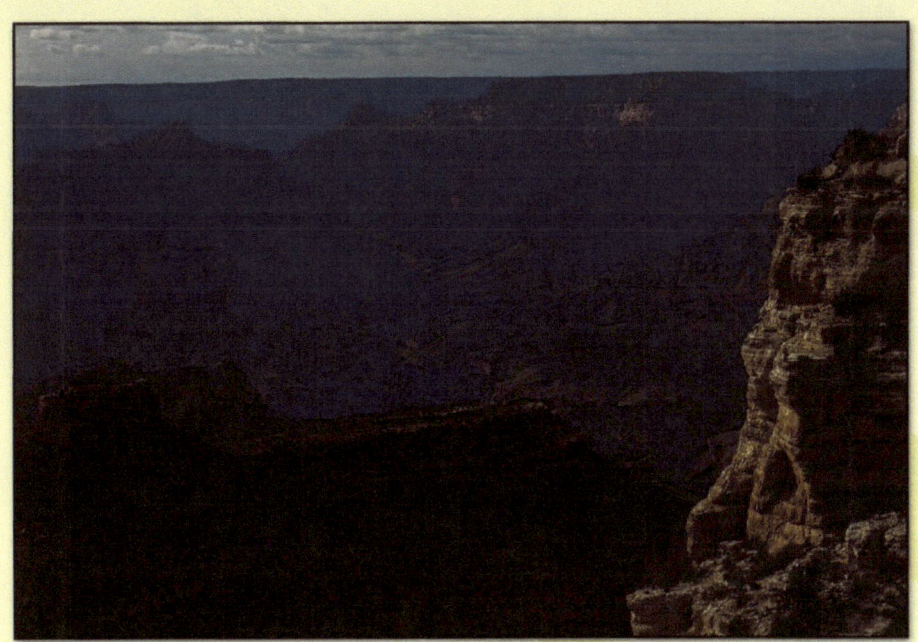

Popular Lookout Points at the Grand Canyon

There are so many great lookout points throughout Grand Canyon National Park, one would need to visit the area for at least a month to be able to visit them all!

Here is a breakdown of the rims most popular spots to view the canyon:

Views from the South Rim	Views from the North Rim
Mather Point	Bright Angel Point
Lookout Studio	Point Imperial
Yavapai Point	Cape Royal
Desert Watchtower	Toroweap Overlook
Lipan Point	Vista Encantada
Moran Point	Tiyo Point
Yaki Point	Widforss Point
Grandview Point	

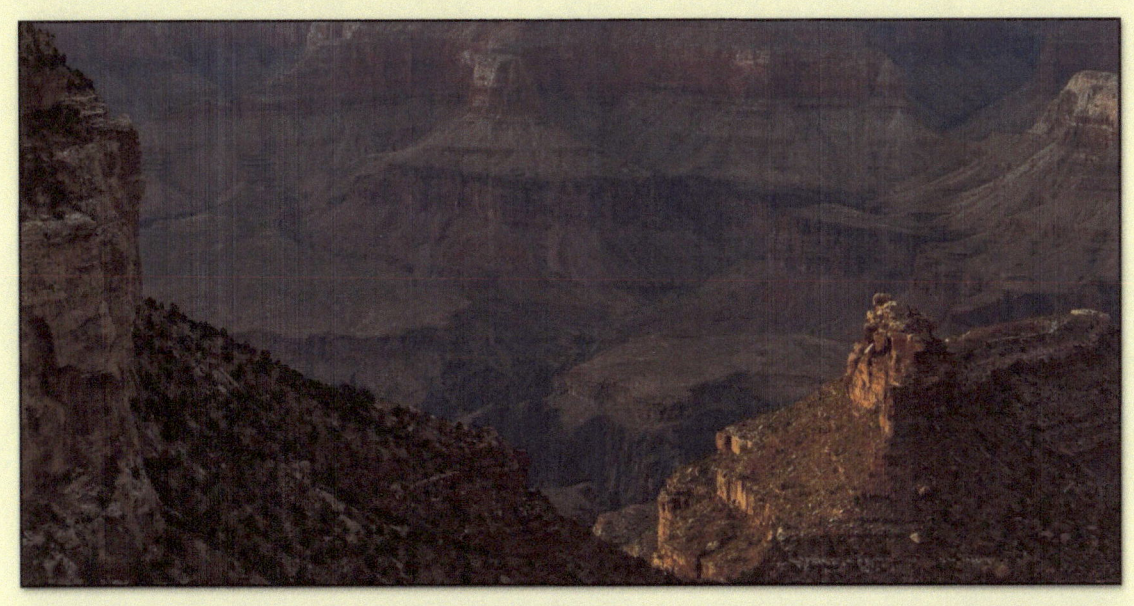

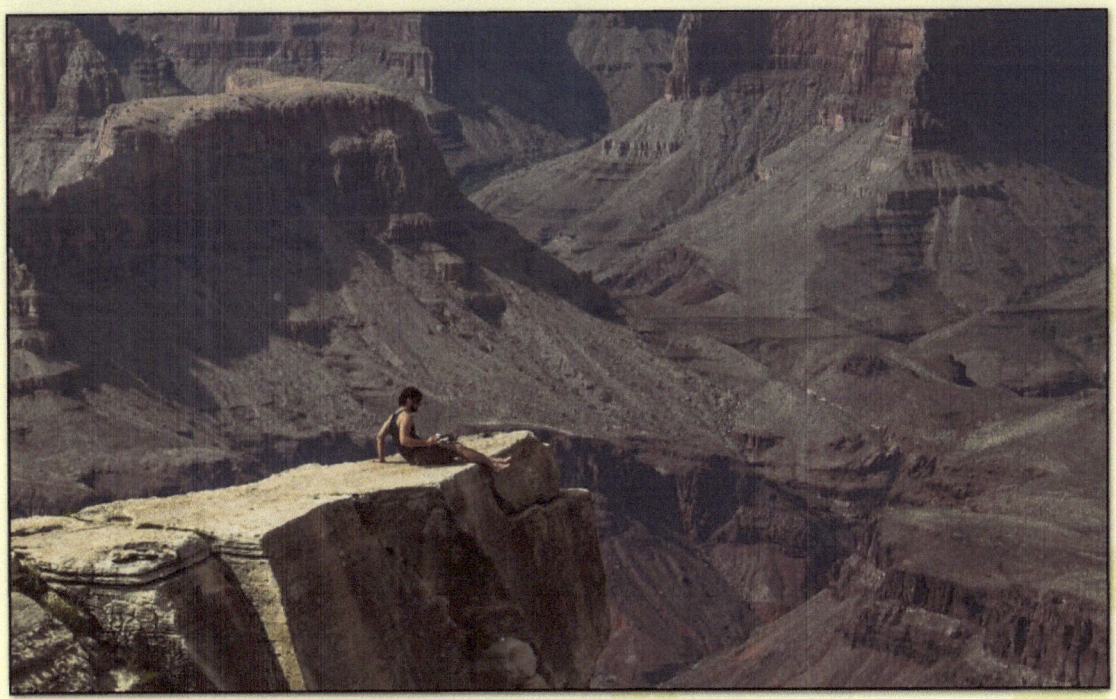

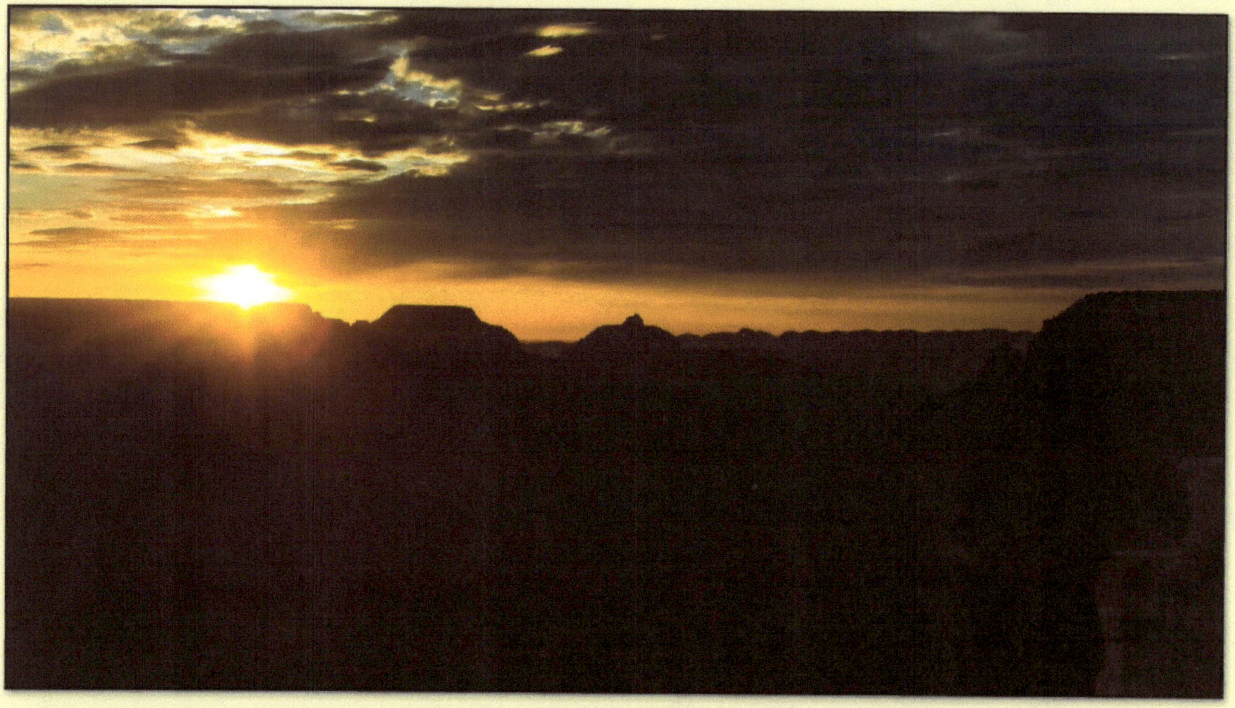

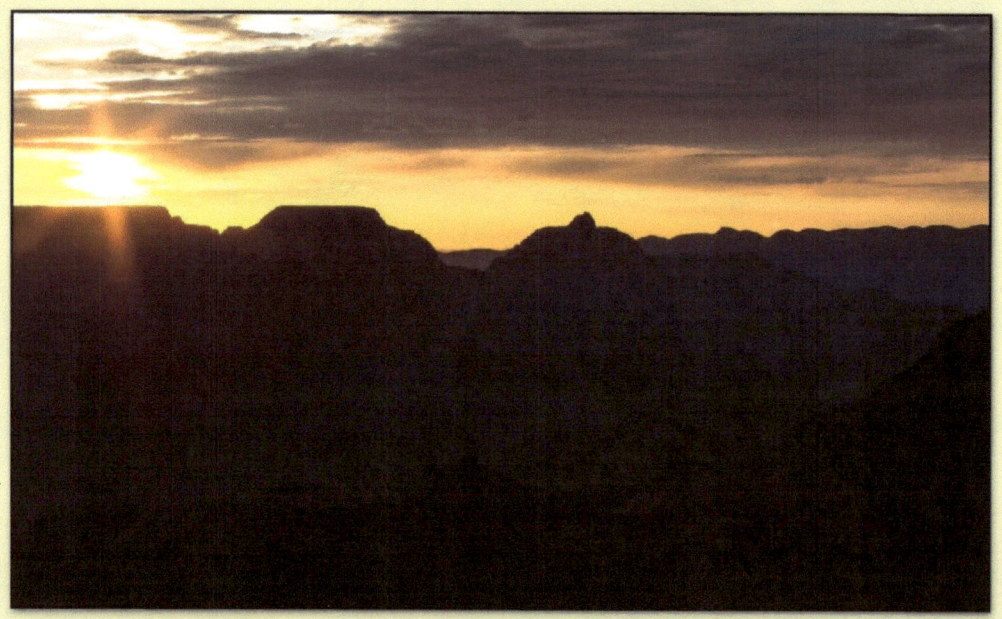

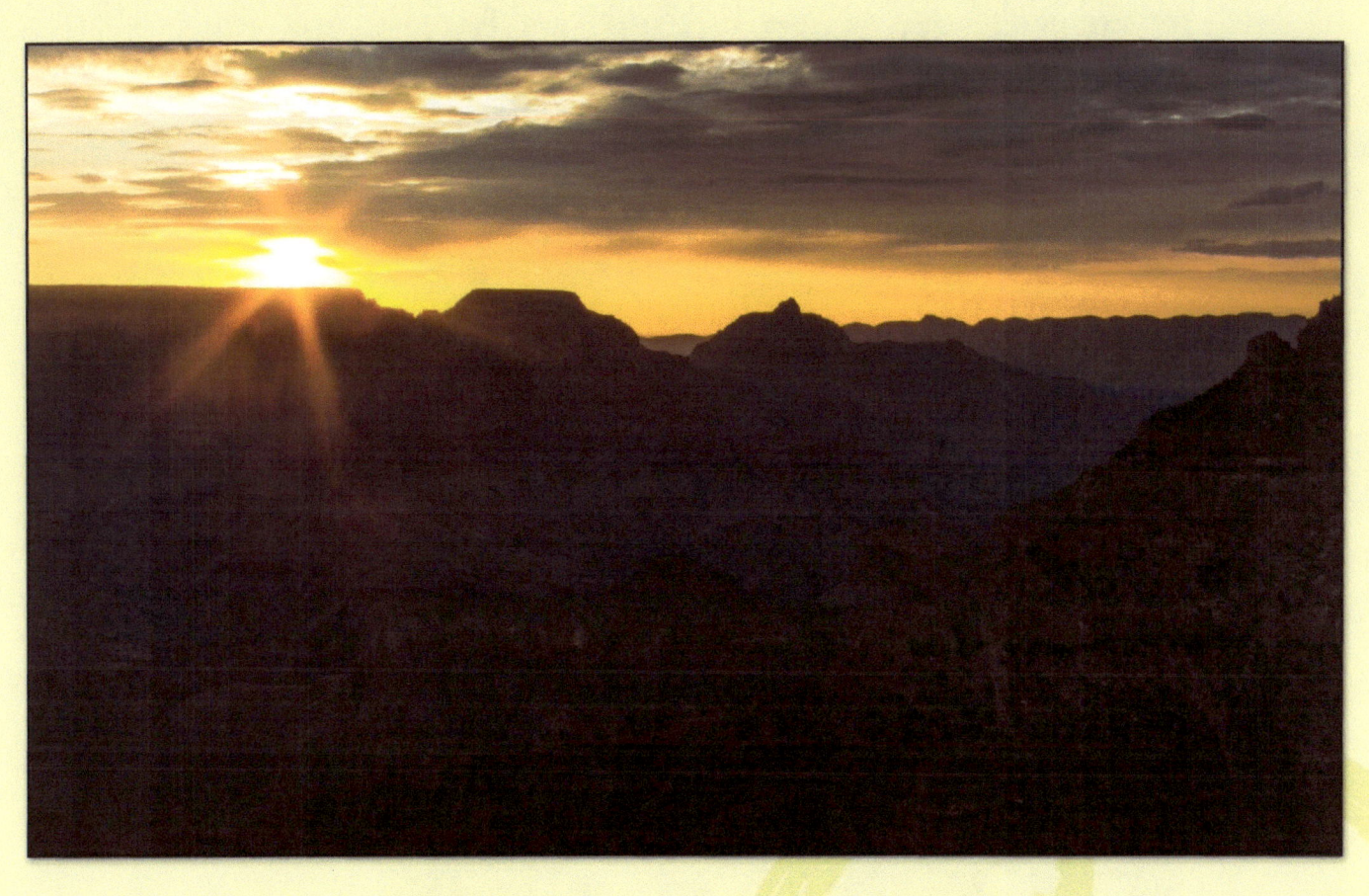

Hiking from Rim to Rim

Are you adventerous? Do you have a lot of endurance? If so, then hiking from the south rim to the North Rim may just be the experience of a lifetime for you.

About a 23 mile hike, most hikers start at the Roaring Springs Canyon located at the North Rim. The beginning of the hike is a journey through a dense evergreen forest, up until the Supai Tunnel, when the trail turns into a desert landscape, where you can see forever.

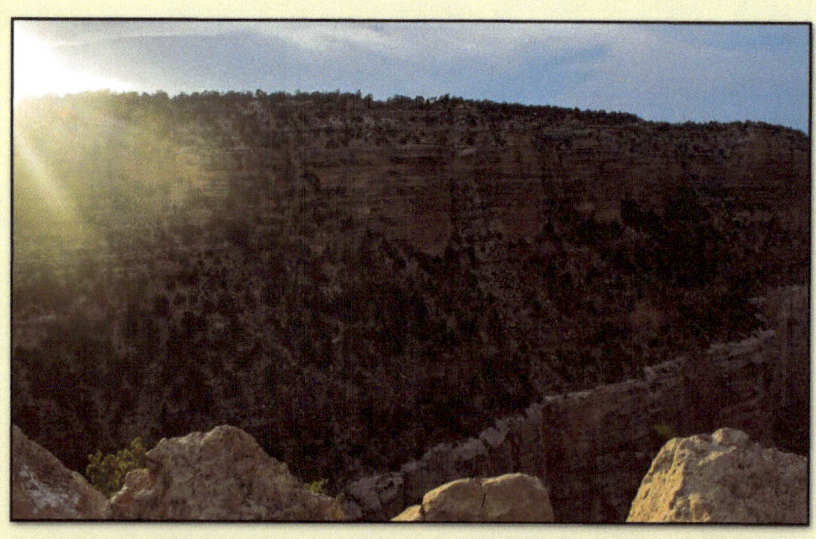

Two miles past the Supai Tunnel you will come across the Roaring Springs, an awe inspiring sight. Continue on down the trail and you will wind up in the Bright Angel Canyon, one of the largest canyons in the entire park.

Just beyond Bright Angel Canyon is Cottonwood Camp, the end of the trail - tap water is available at the camp so you can rehydrate after your hike.

CAUTION: Hiking from rim to rim at the Grand Canyon is dangerous and very difficult. The high altitude, combined with the rapidly changing weather makes the hike very risky. Only attempt this if you are in peak physical condition.

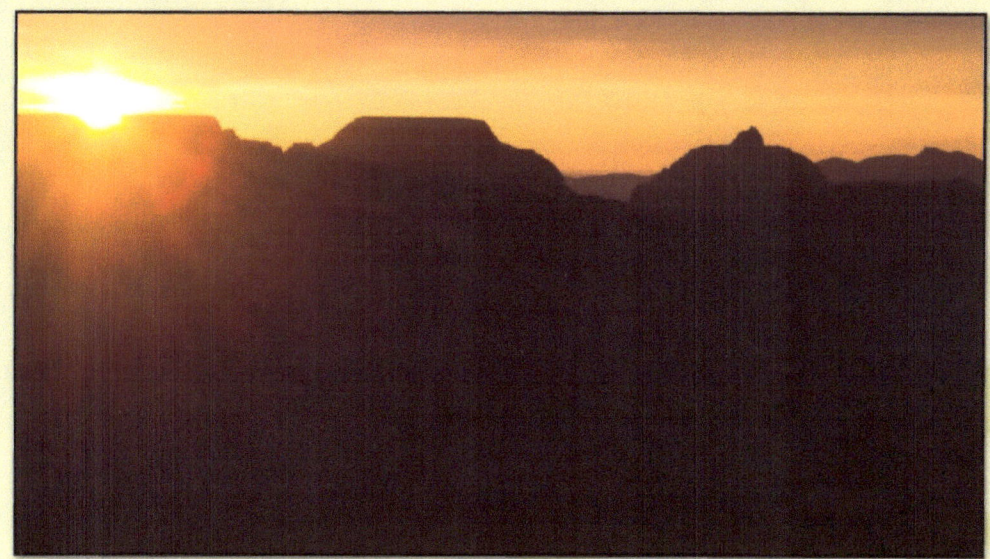

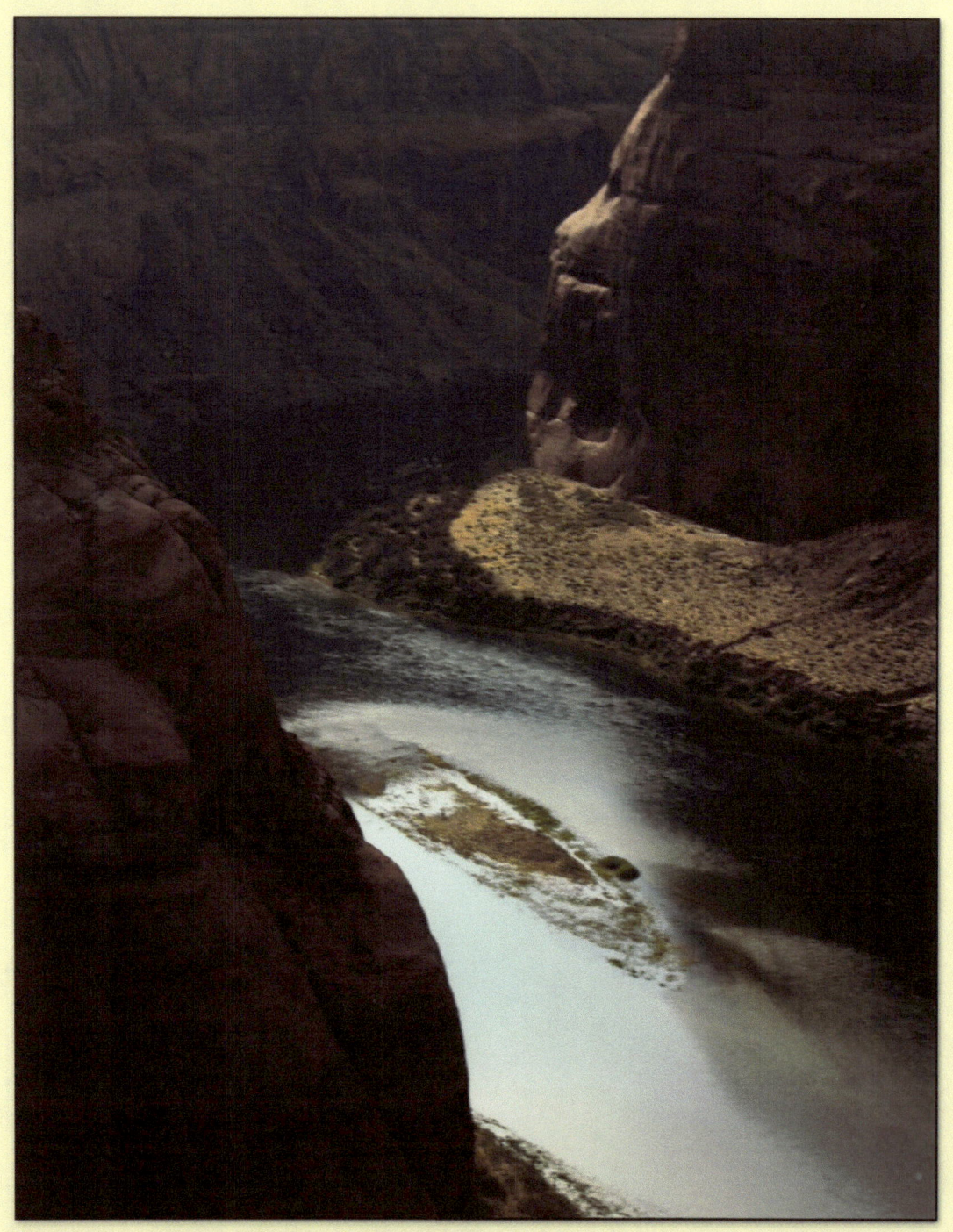

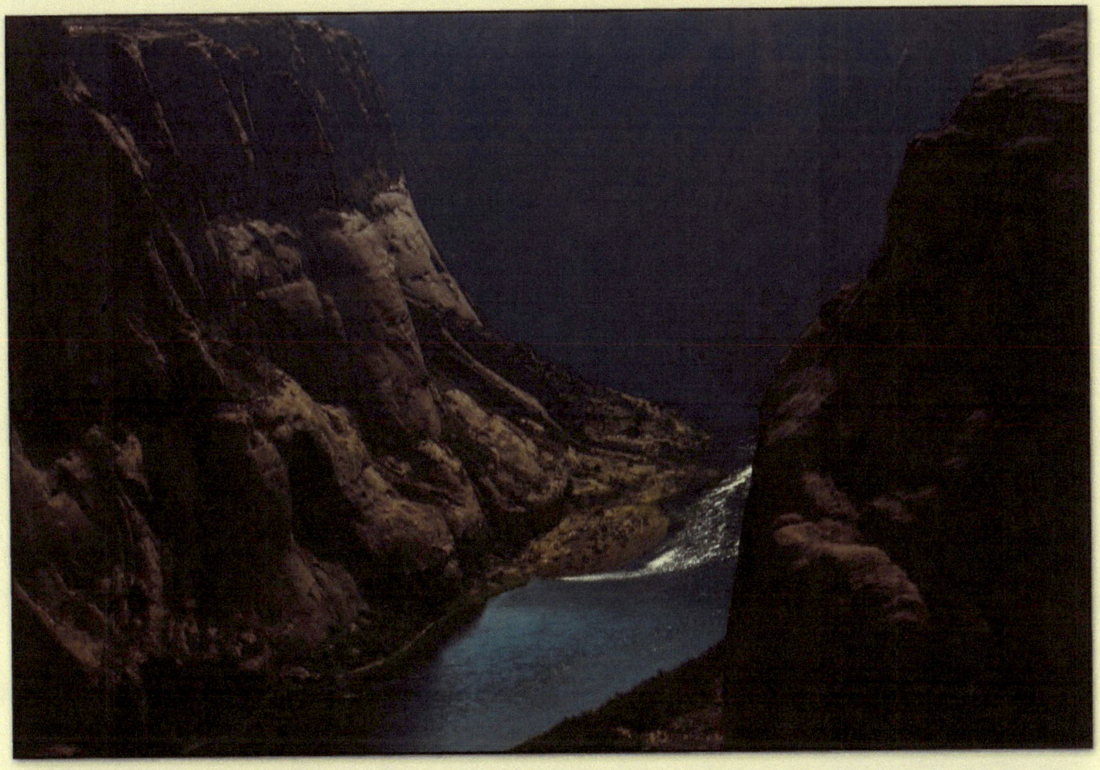

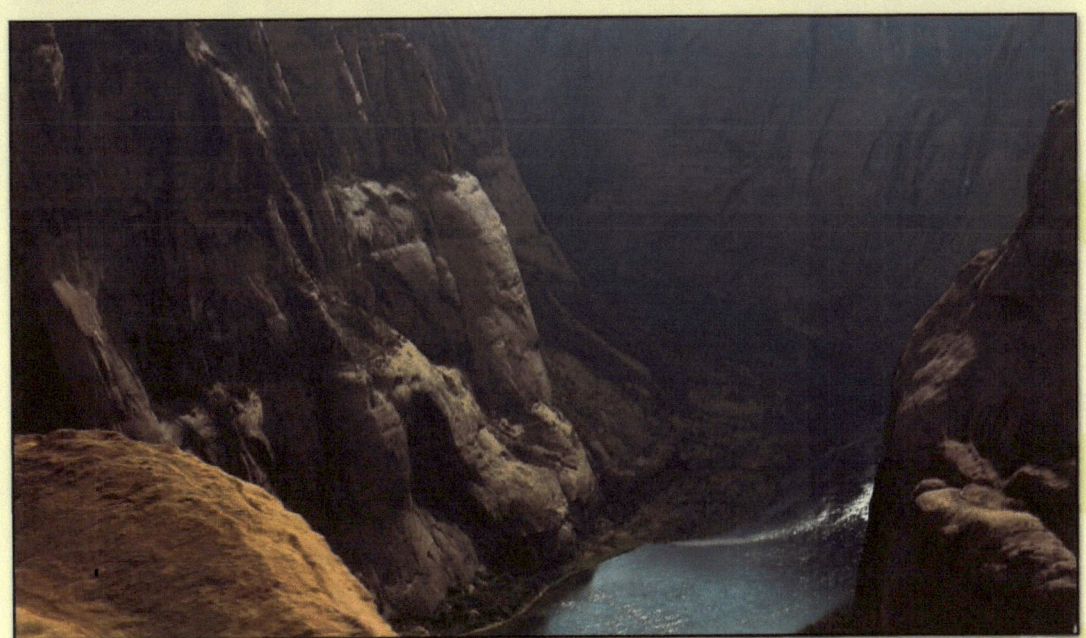

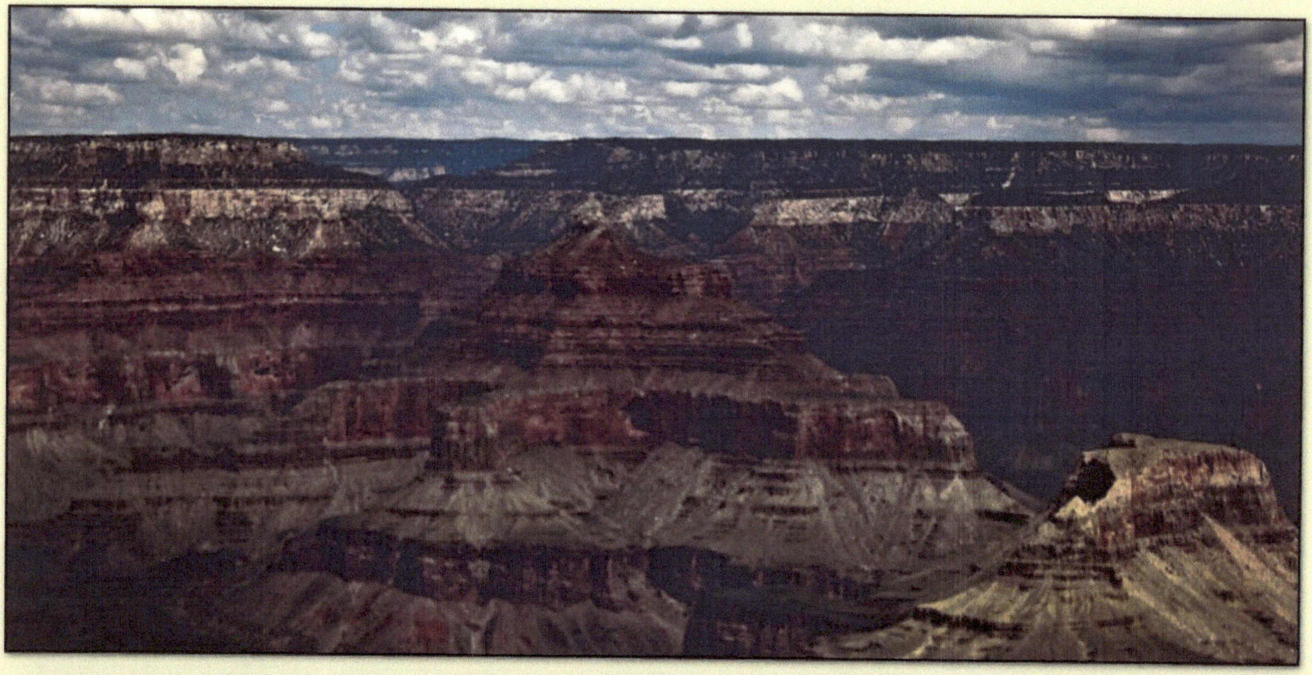

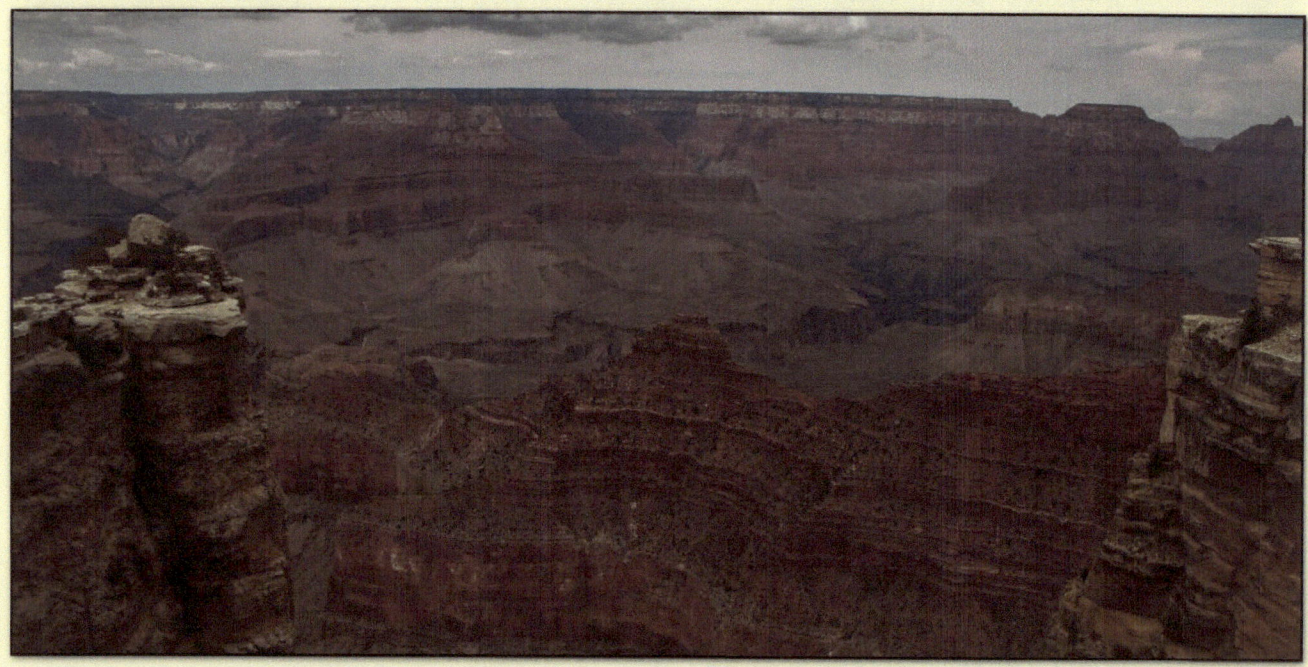

Bright Angel Trail at the Grand Canyon

The most popular hiking trail at Grand Canyon National Park is the Bright Angel Trail.

The trail begins at the visitor center located at the park and offers breathtaking views of the canyon, plenty of rest stops, and water fountains to keep you hydrated while you are taking in the beautiful view.

The trail is broken up into sections to make it easy for hikers of all experience levels. The shortest trail is three miles, the next distance is 4.5 miles, and the total trail is thirteen miles long.

If you are going to hike any of the trails be sure to bring plenty of water, sunscreen and energy, because the elevation at Bright Angel Point is just under 7,000 feet!

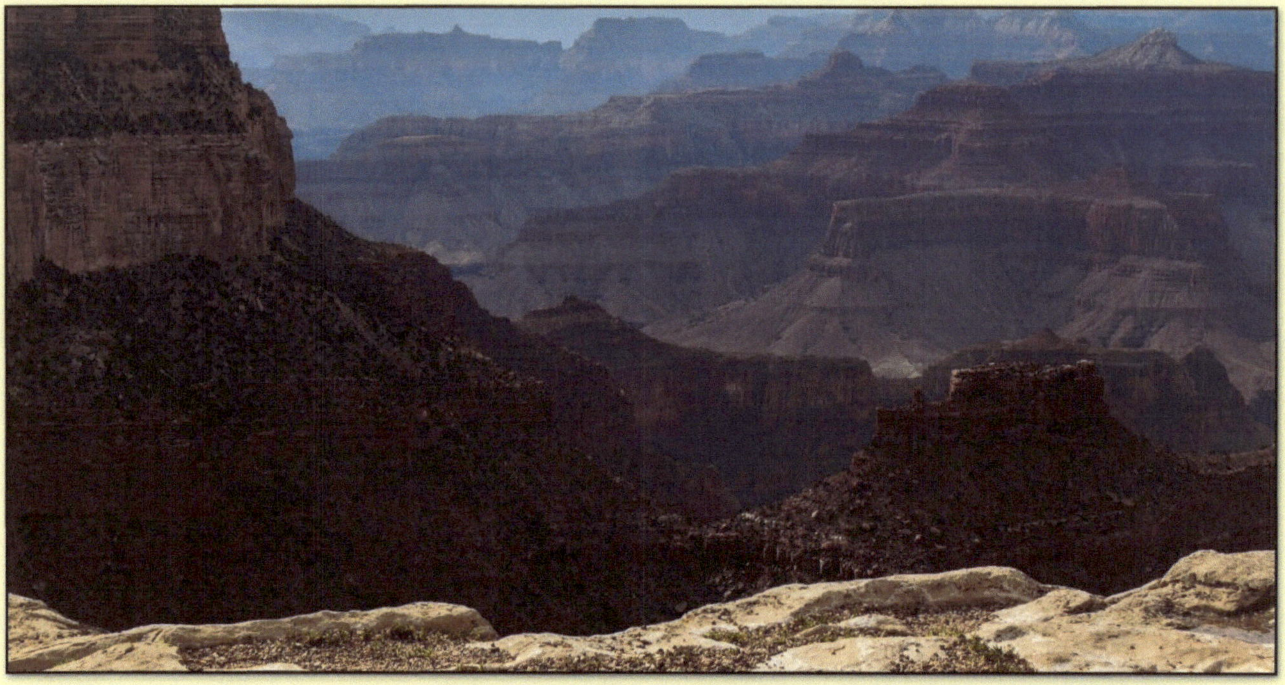

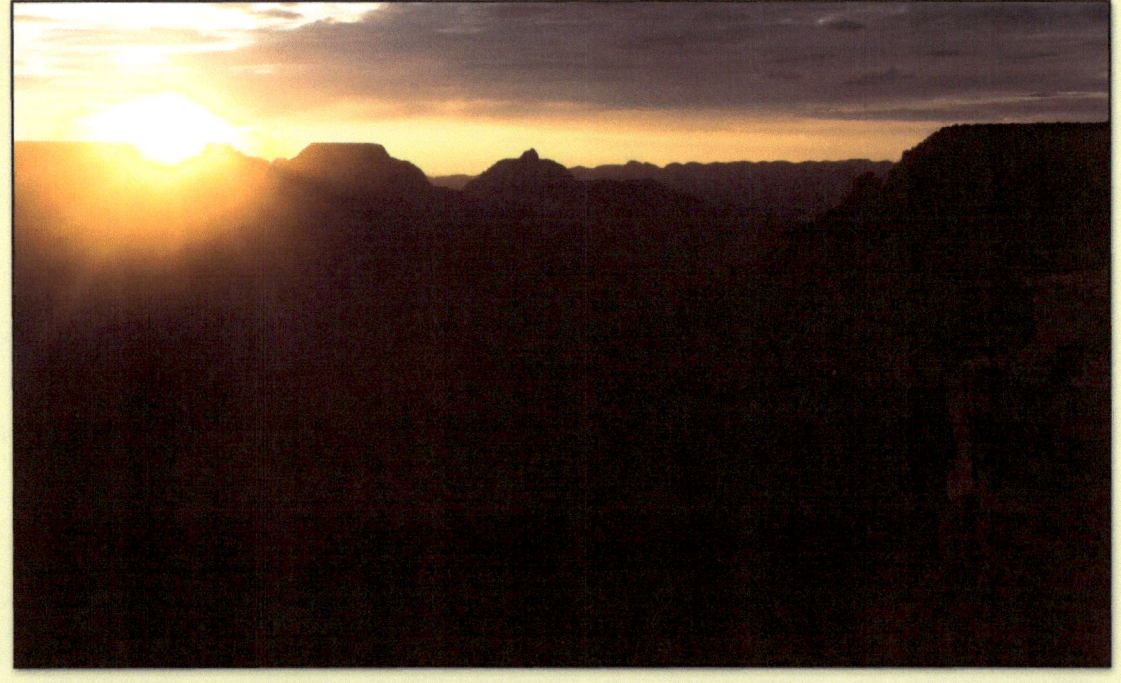

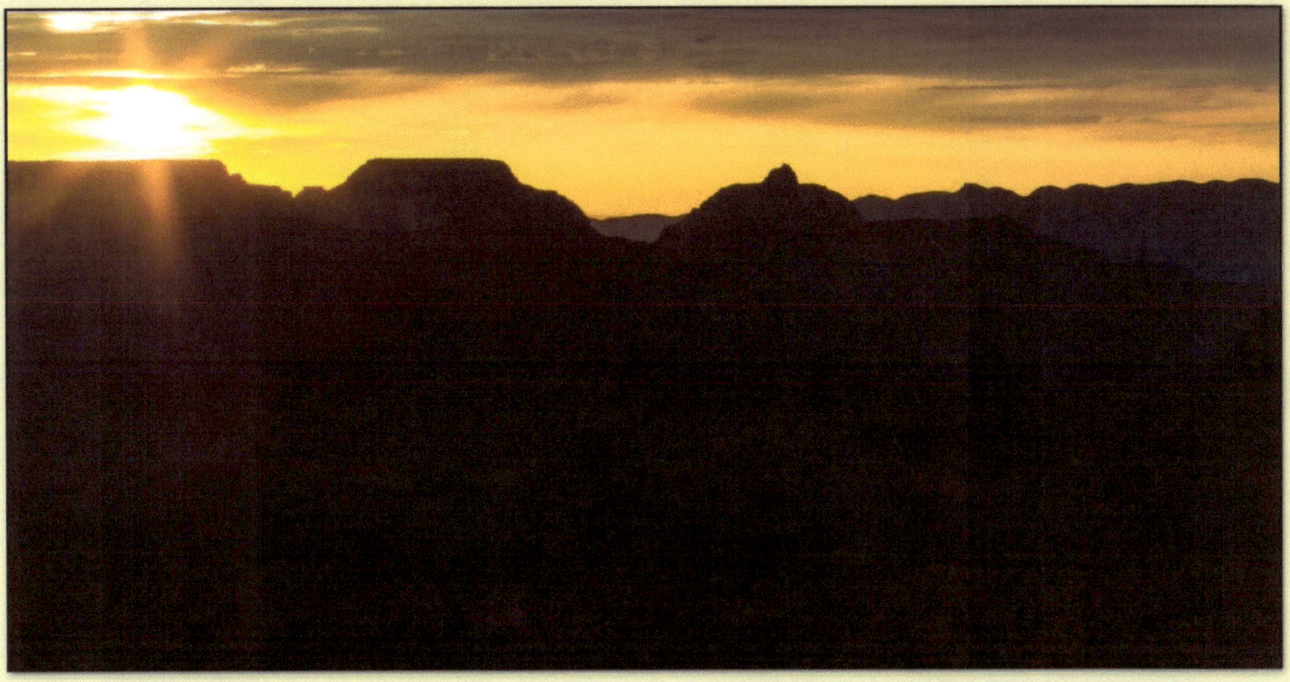

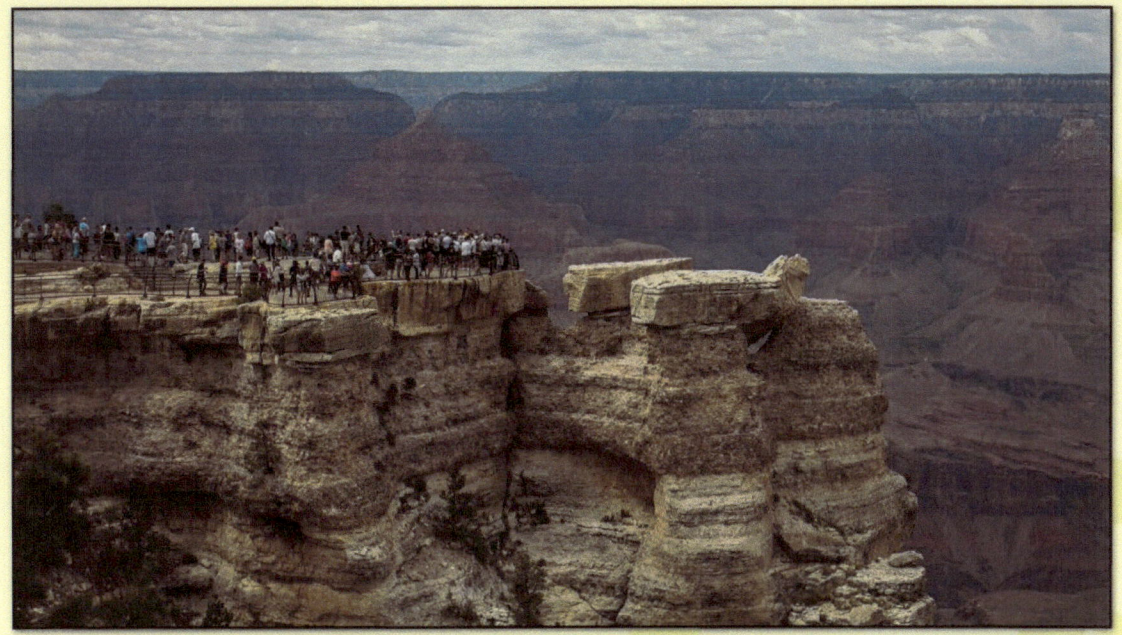

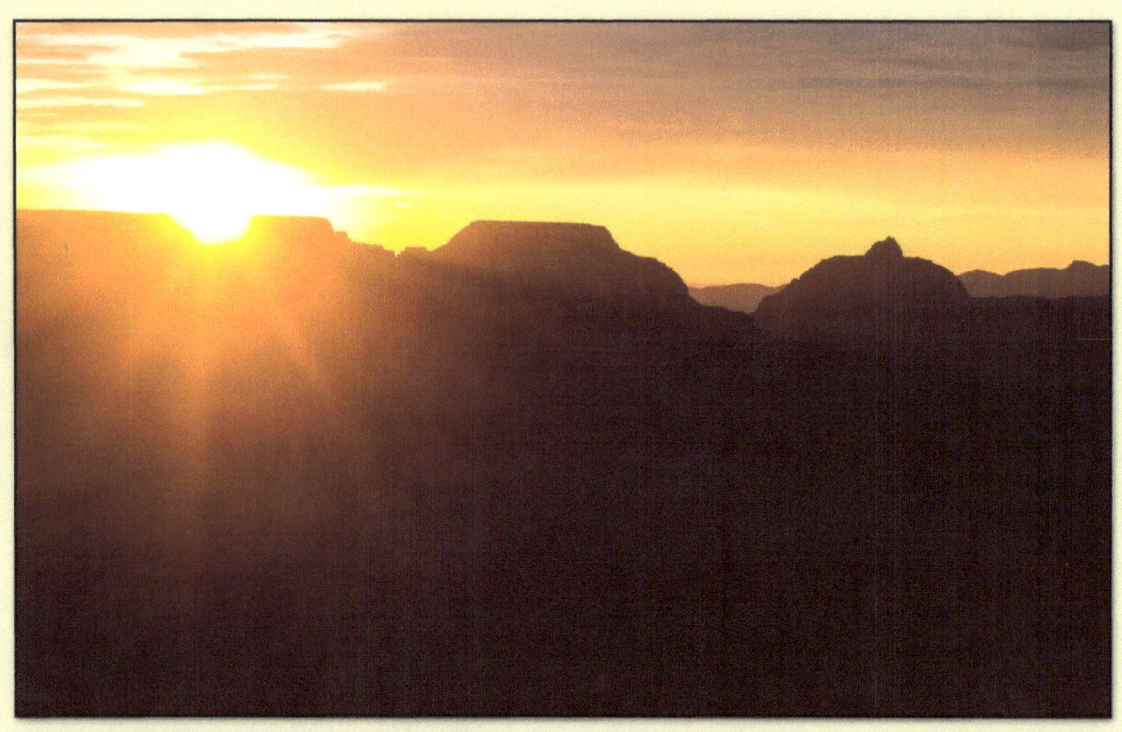
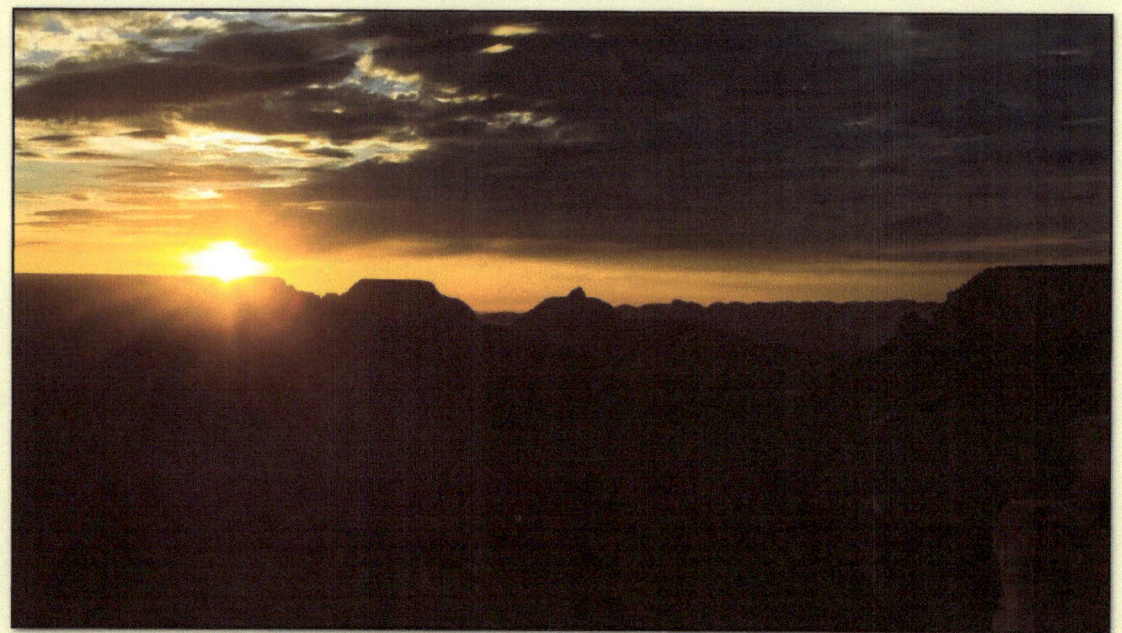

Mathers Point in Grand Canyon National Park

If you are visiting the Grand Canyon because of the scenery, then you need to know the best place to watch the sunrise and sunset at the park. That location is Mathers Point.

Two and a half miles north of the entrance to the park at the South Rim, Mathers Point offers stunning, jaw-dropping views of the canyon. Mathers Point is at the edge of a cliff extending into the canyon, allowing for panaromic views of the park.

The view from Mathers Point is especially beautiful when the sun is rising, because you get to witness a thick bed of fog rise from the canyons along with the sun. It is a once in a lifetime experience, and well worth waking up at 4 o' clock in the morning!

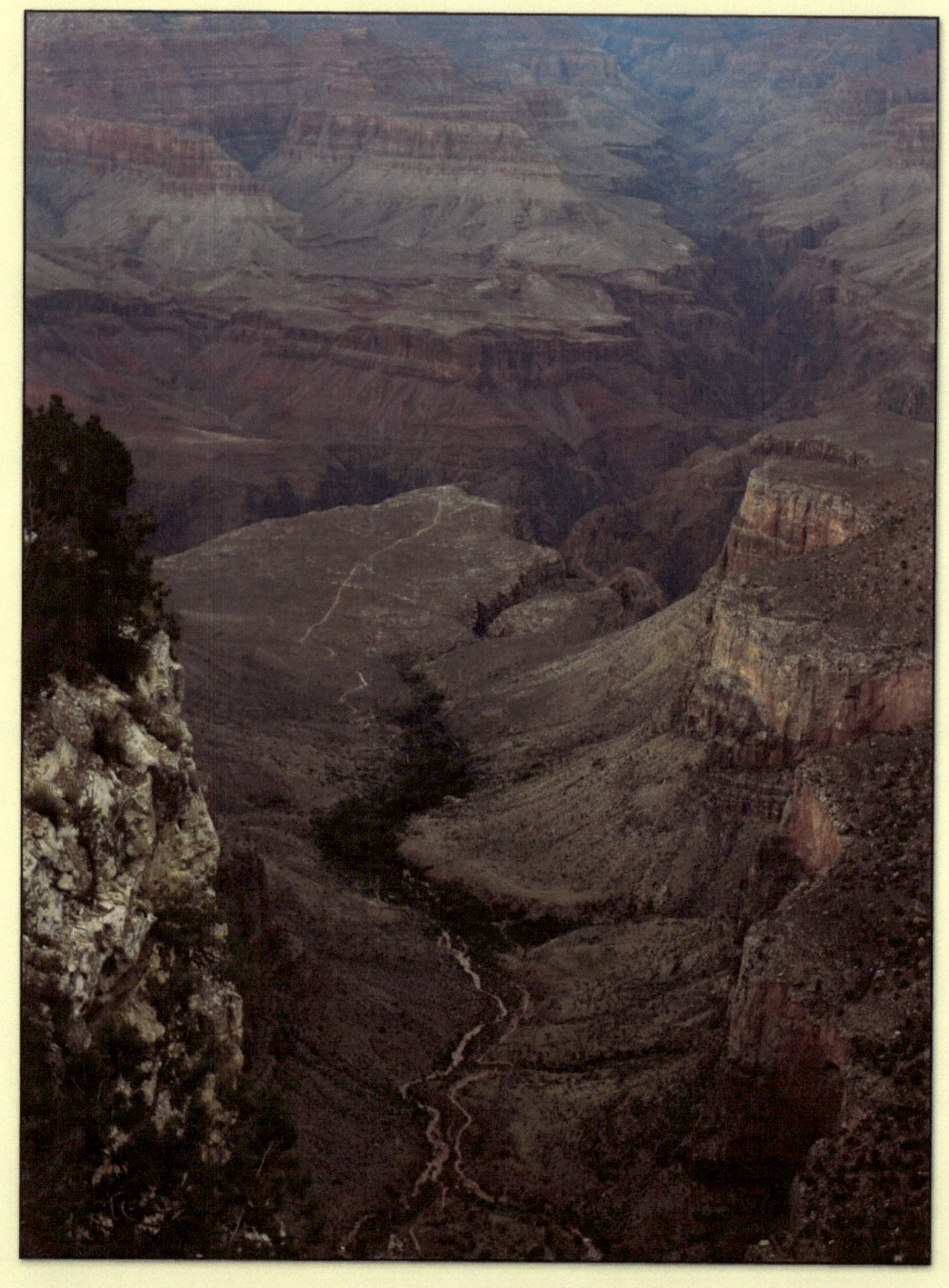

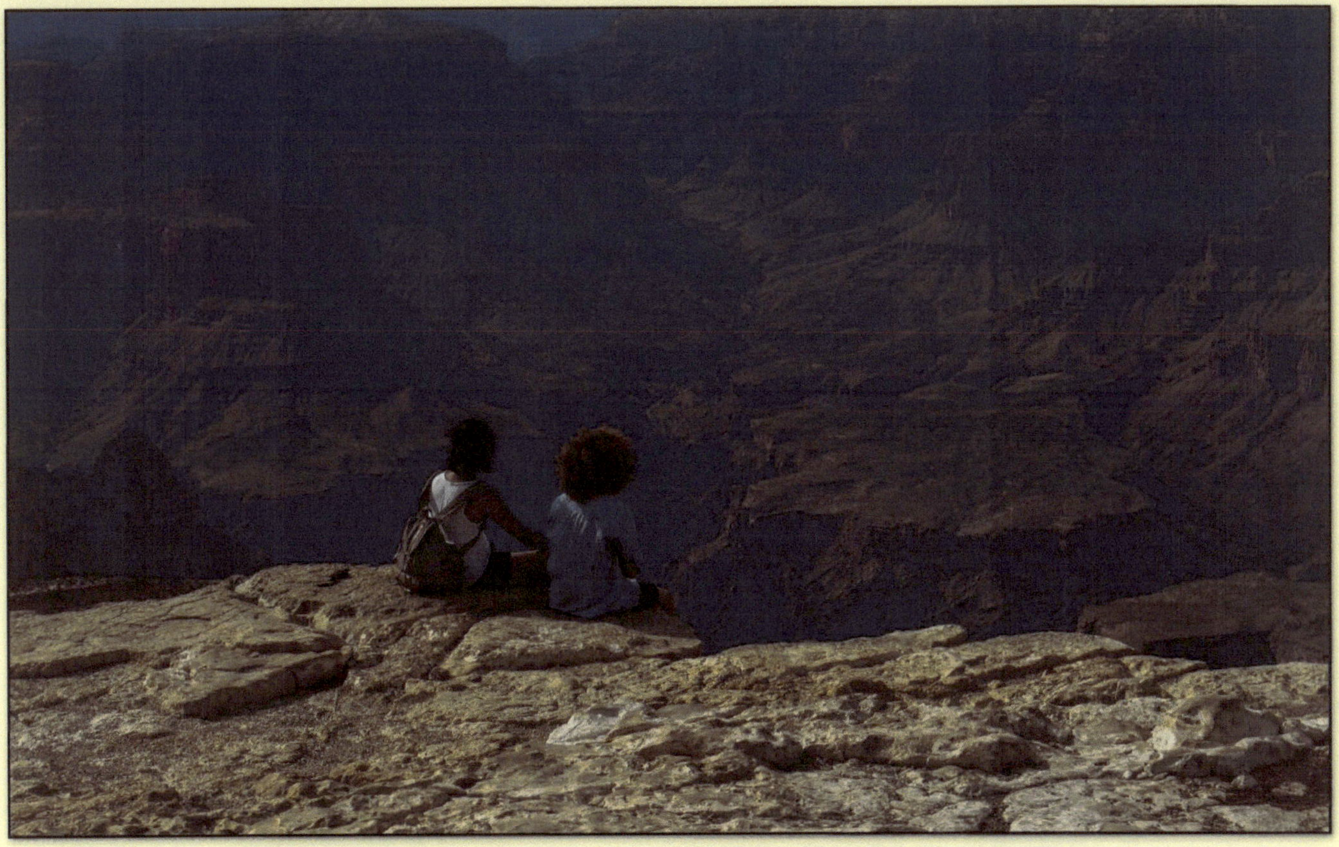

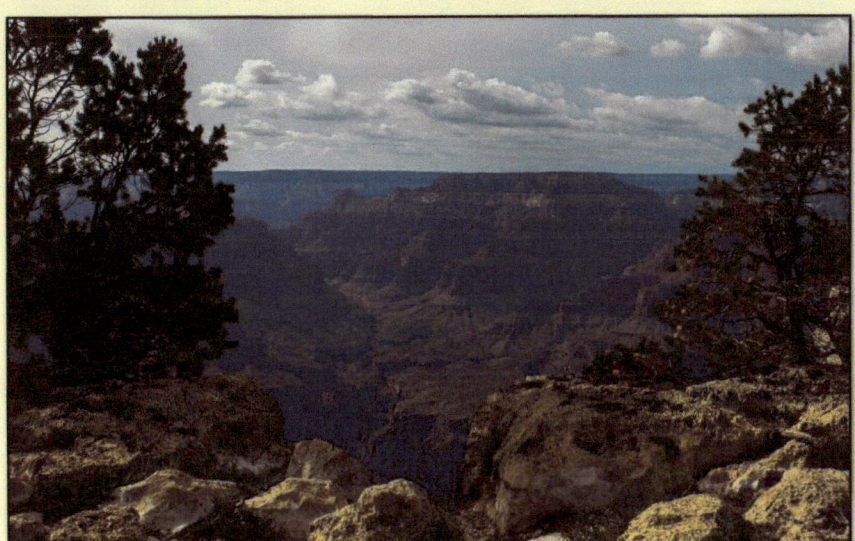

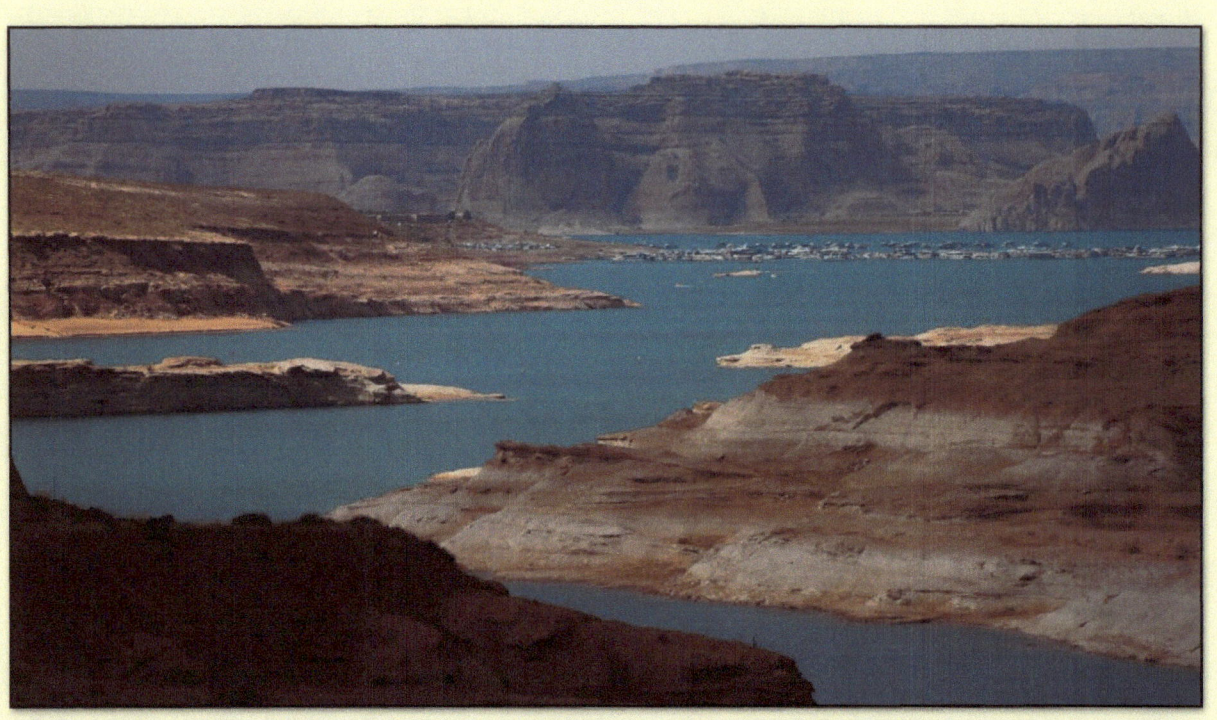

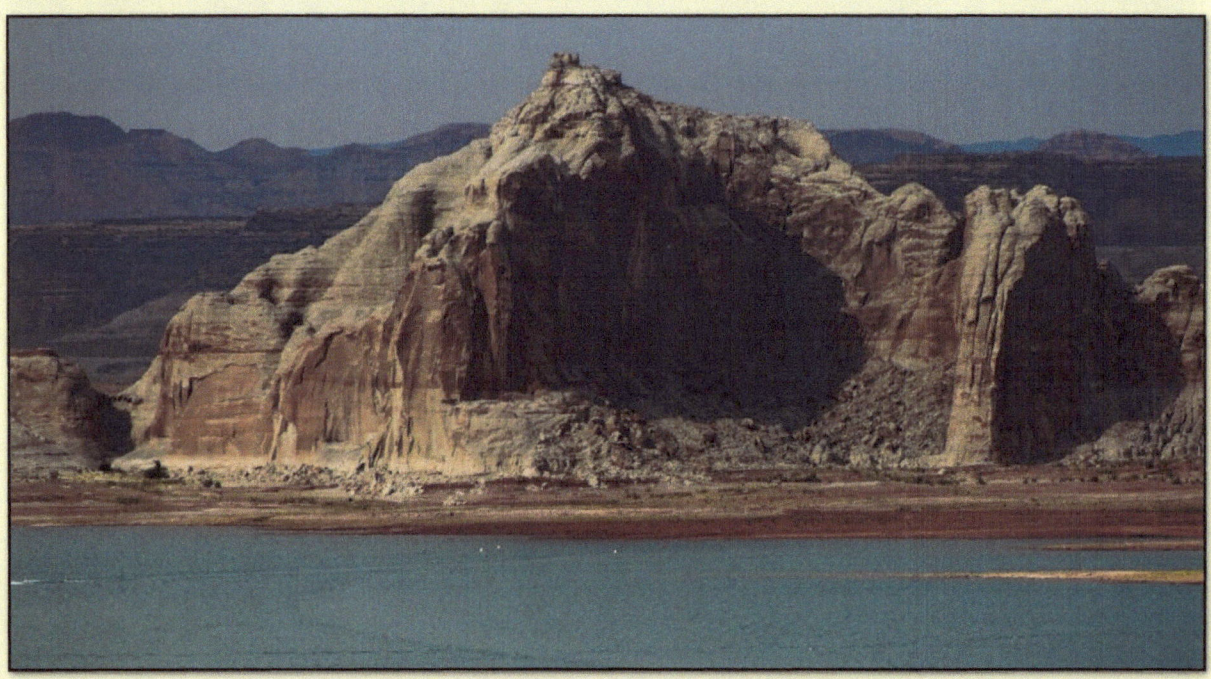

White Water Rafting on the Colorado River

Once you are tired of hiking, head down to the Colorado River for some white water rafting! At the canyon you have three options, full canyon rafting, upper canyon rafting and lower canyon rafting.

Whichever you choose, you are in for a terrific experience and a distinctive view you won't find anywhere else! From rafting trips that last half a day, to trips that last an entire week, rafting down the Colorado River is truly an experience you will never forget.

If you are interested in planned iteneraries containing a mixture of rafting and hiking over several days, check out Grand Canyon Whitewater, the best multi-day rafting tour at the Grand Canyon. For those looking for half day rafting trips or full day rafting trips, Colorado River Discovery offers a variety of great packages for individuals, as well as families.

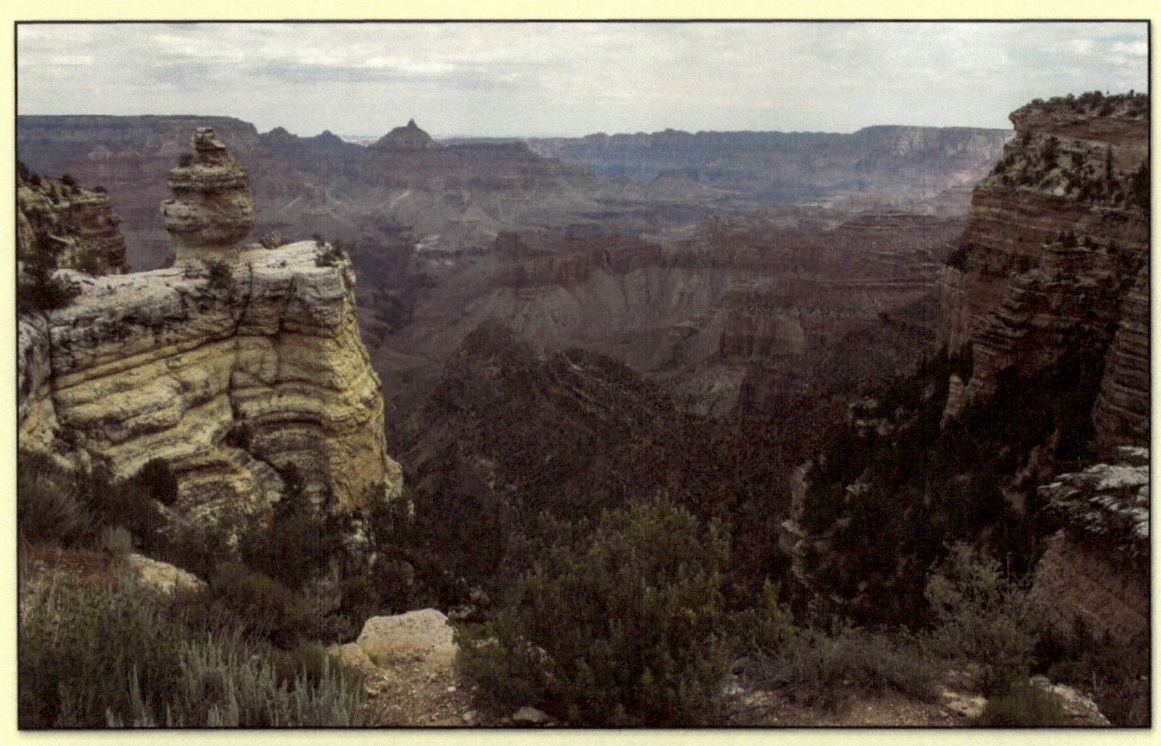

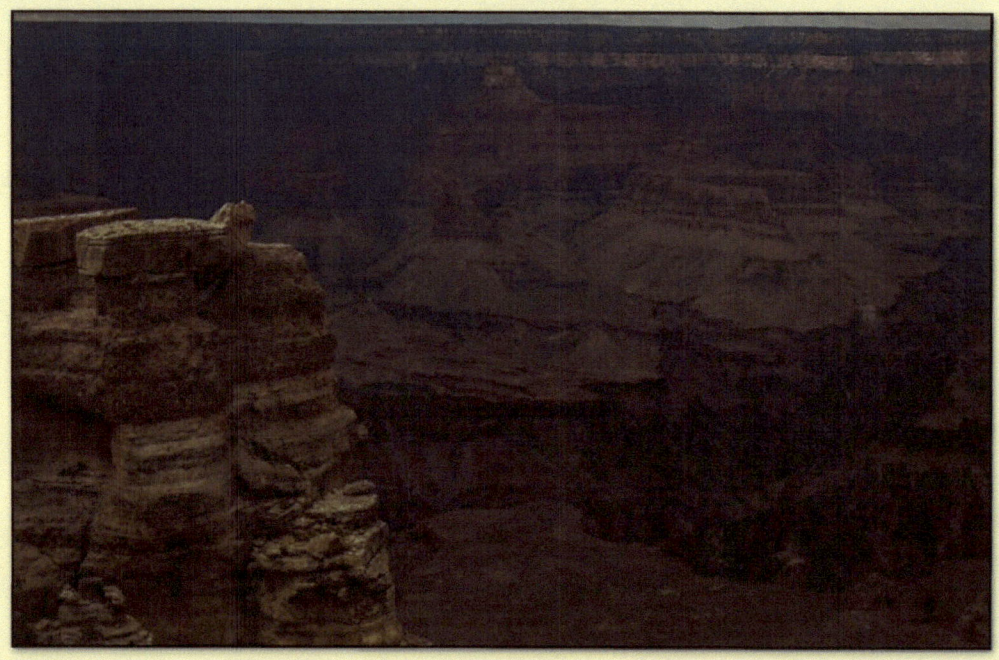

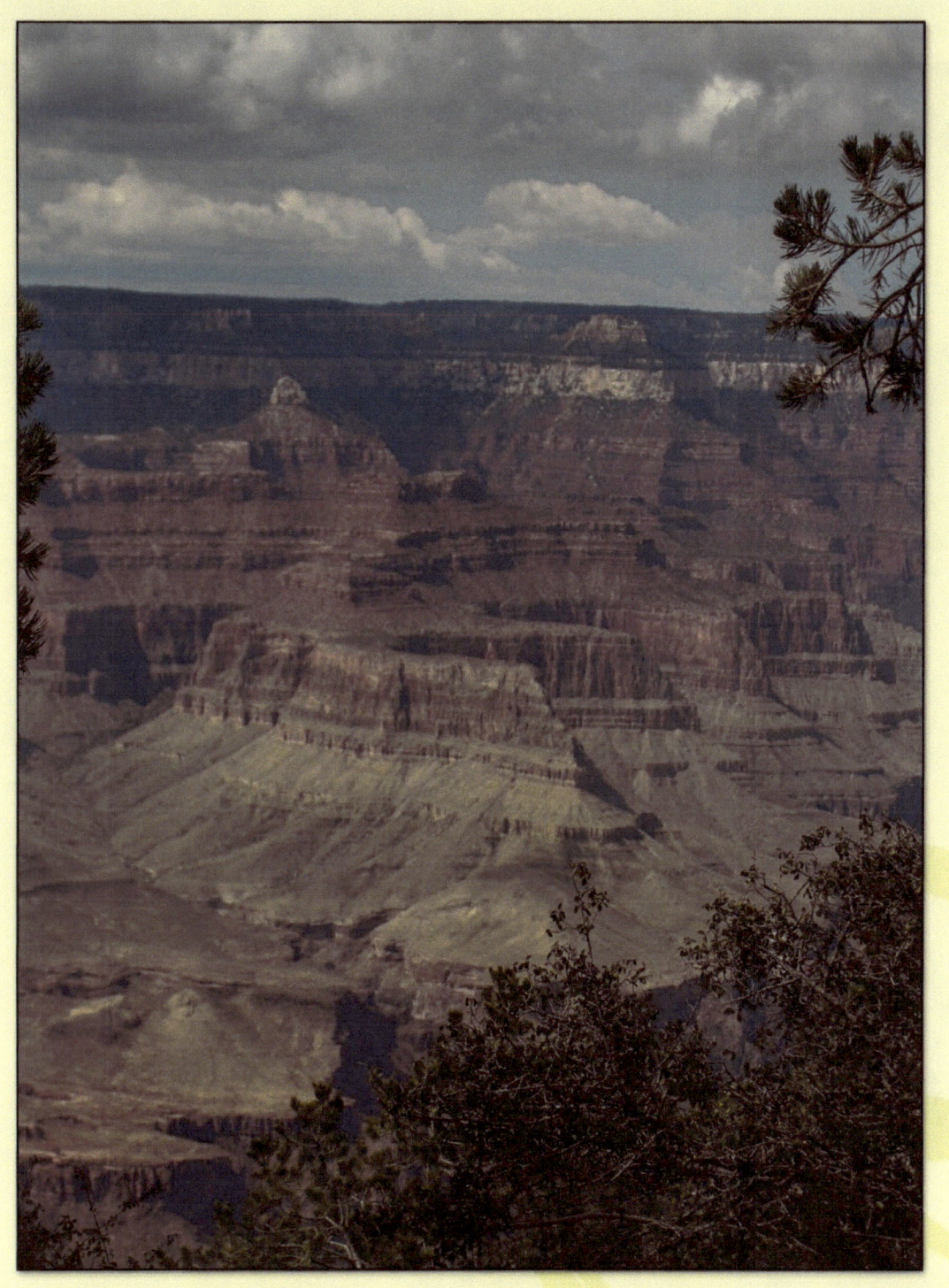

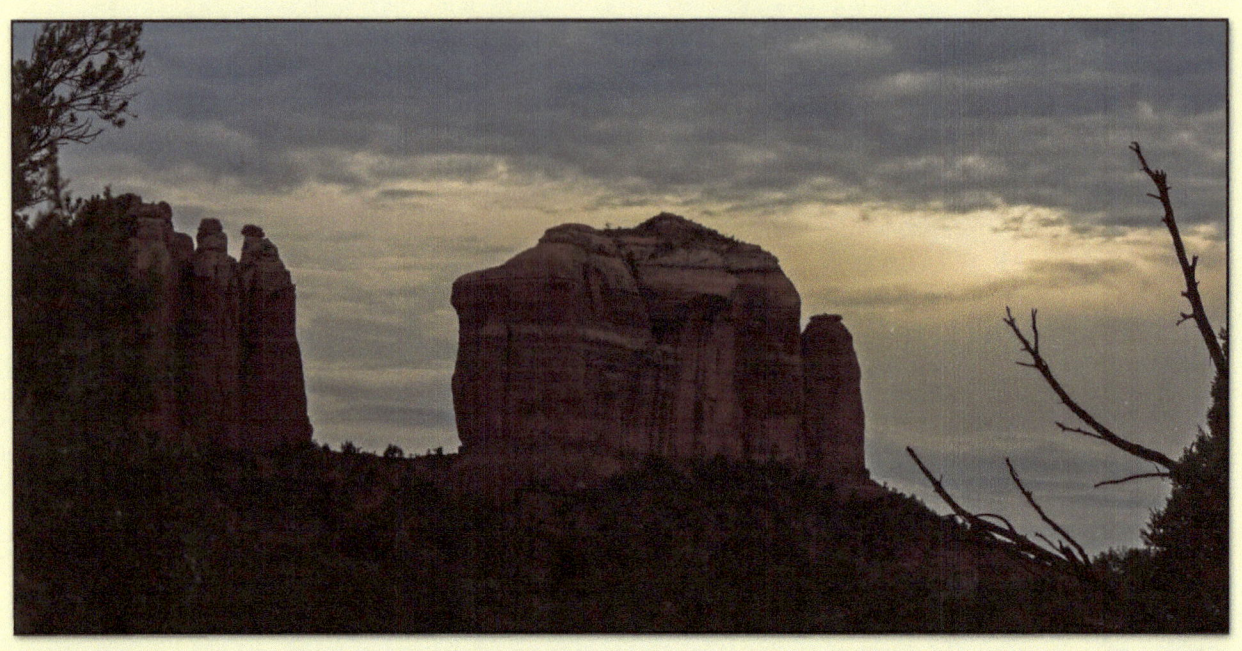

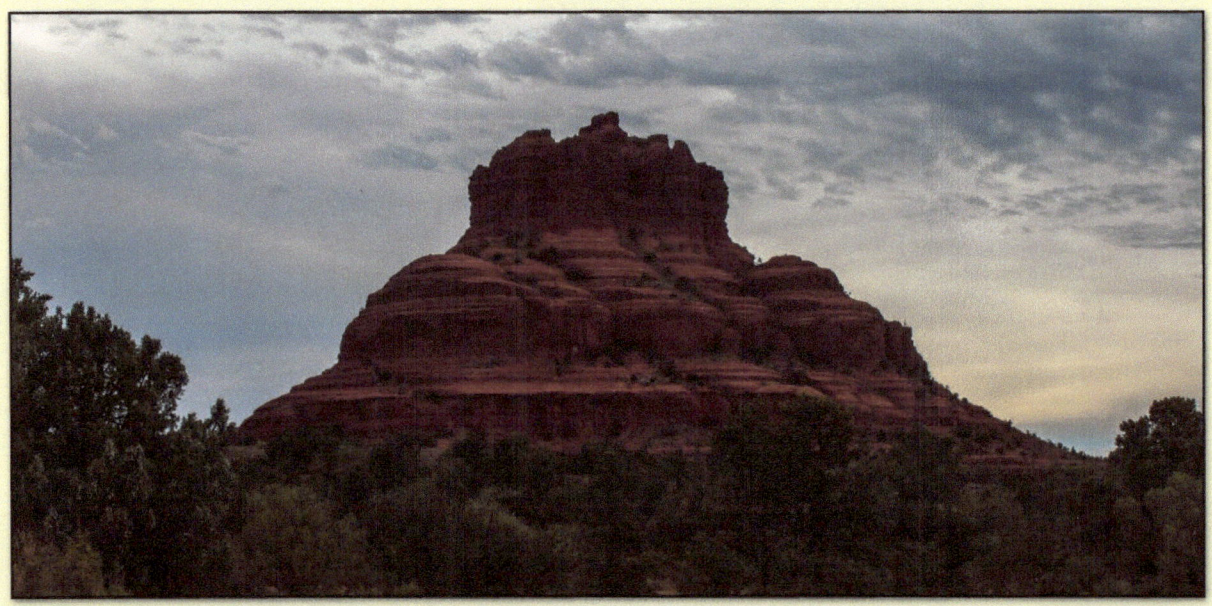

Explore a Secret Canyon

Sedona, Arizona is a beautiful town within driving distance of Grand Canyon National Park.

Filled with quaint restaurants, eccentric shops and beautiful scenery, Sedona is a great place to visit while staying at the Grand Canyon.

The Secret Canyon, located in Sedona, is a ten mile long canyon. It is a great place to go hiking, horseback riding, donkey riding, bike riding, or exploring. If you don't want to exert yourself too much, there is plenty to take in without traveling very far, so don't worry!

Sedona is famous for its rich red rocks which comprise the Secret Canyon, and it is an absolutely breathtaking place to visit.

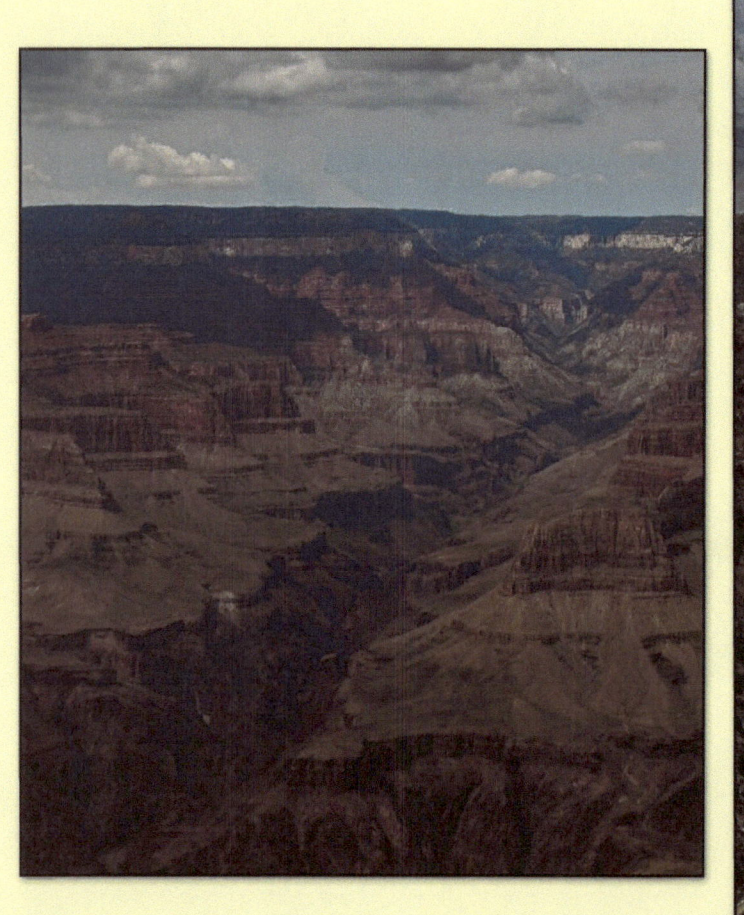
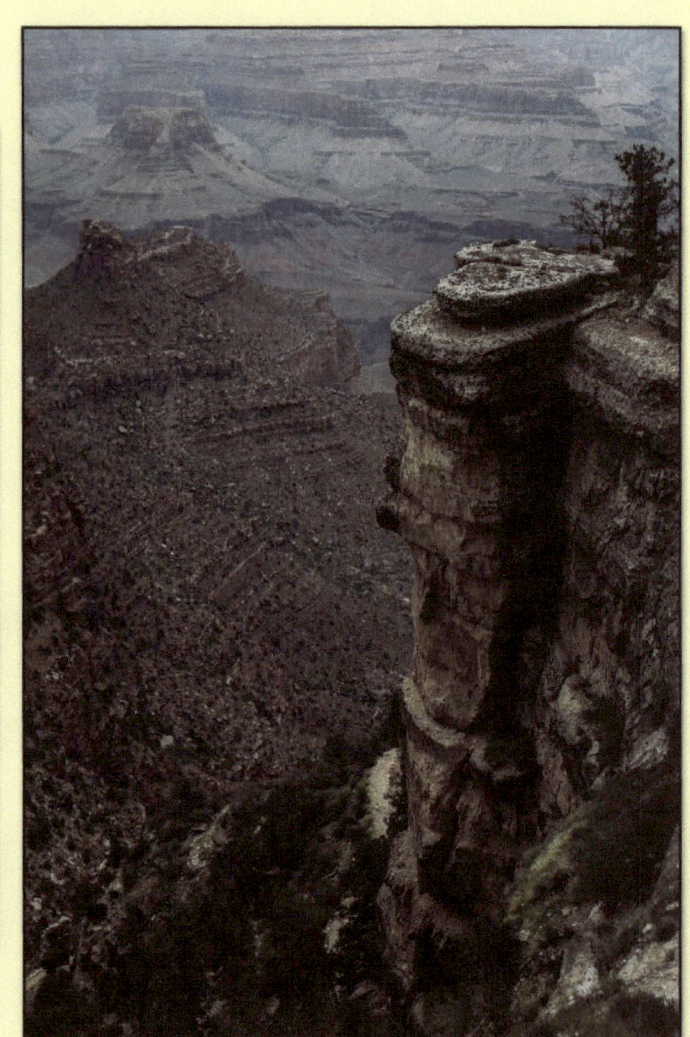

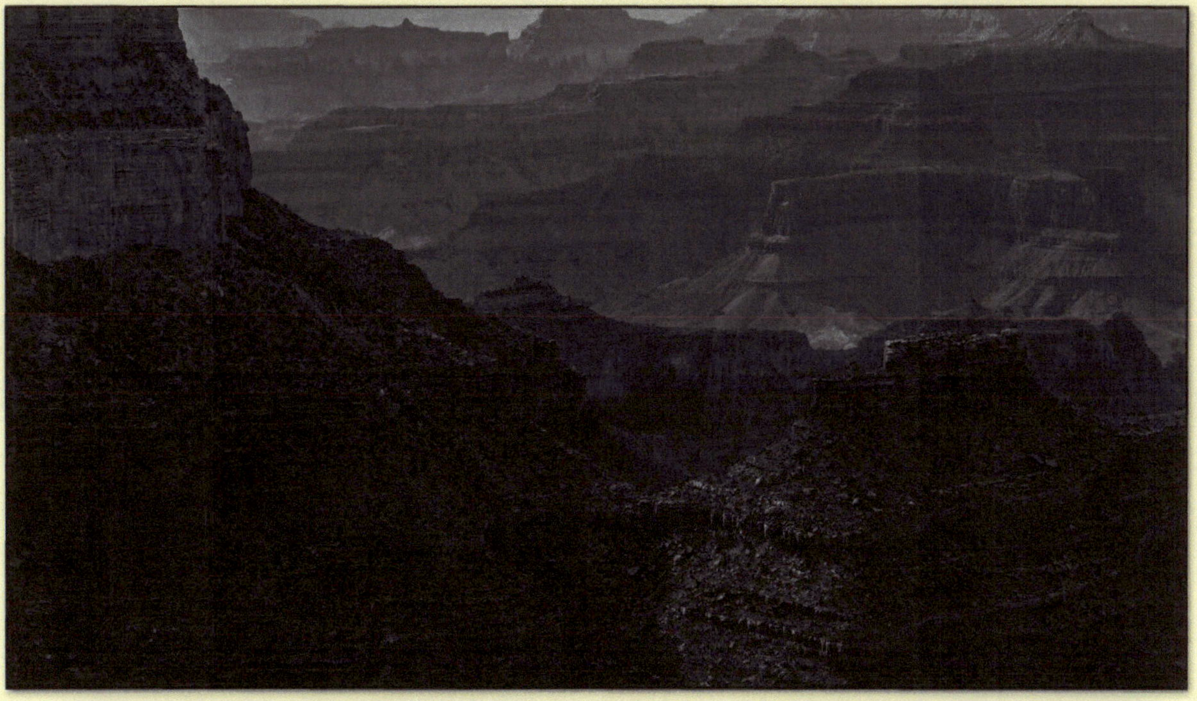

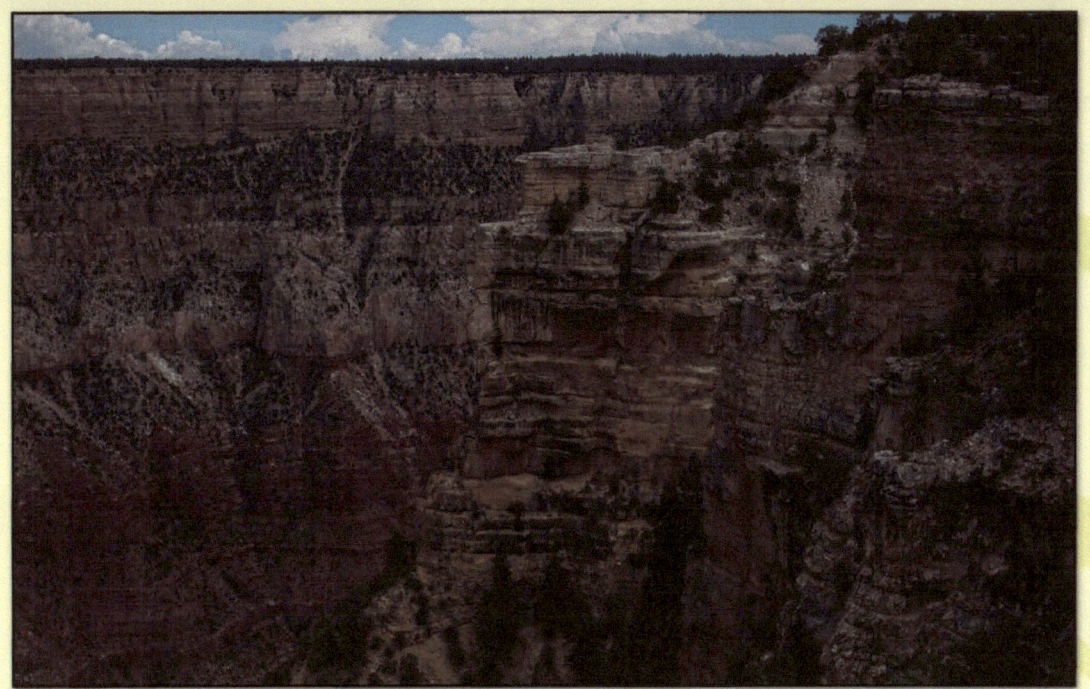

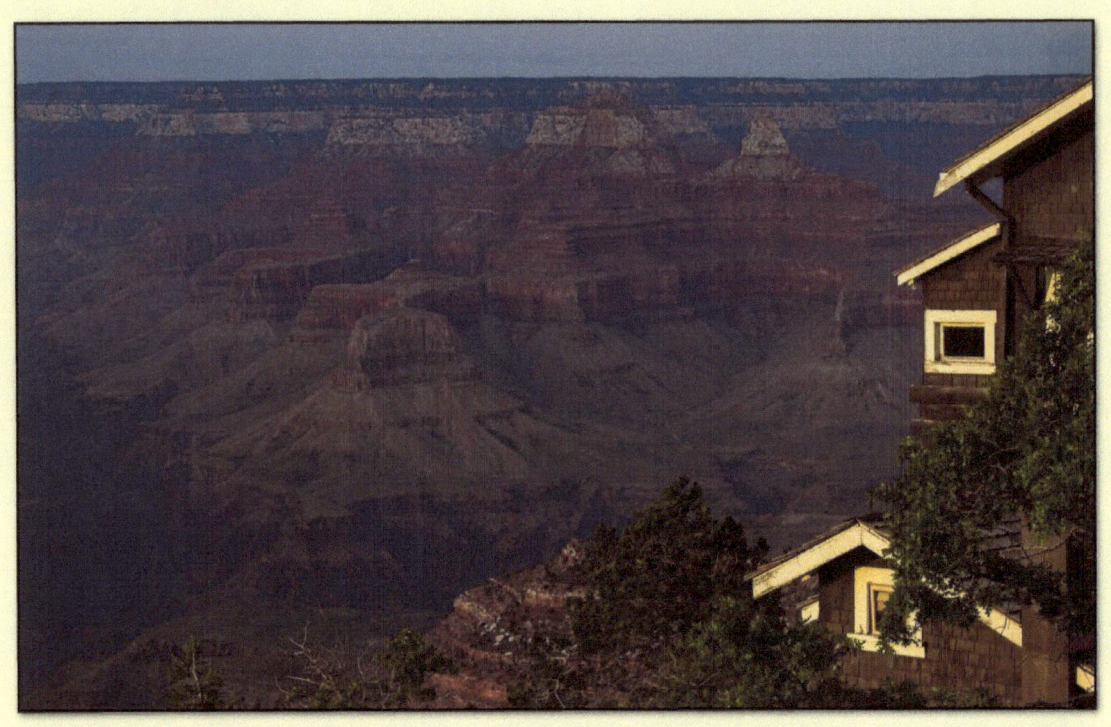

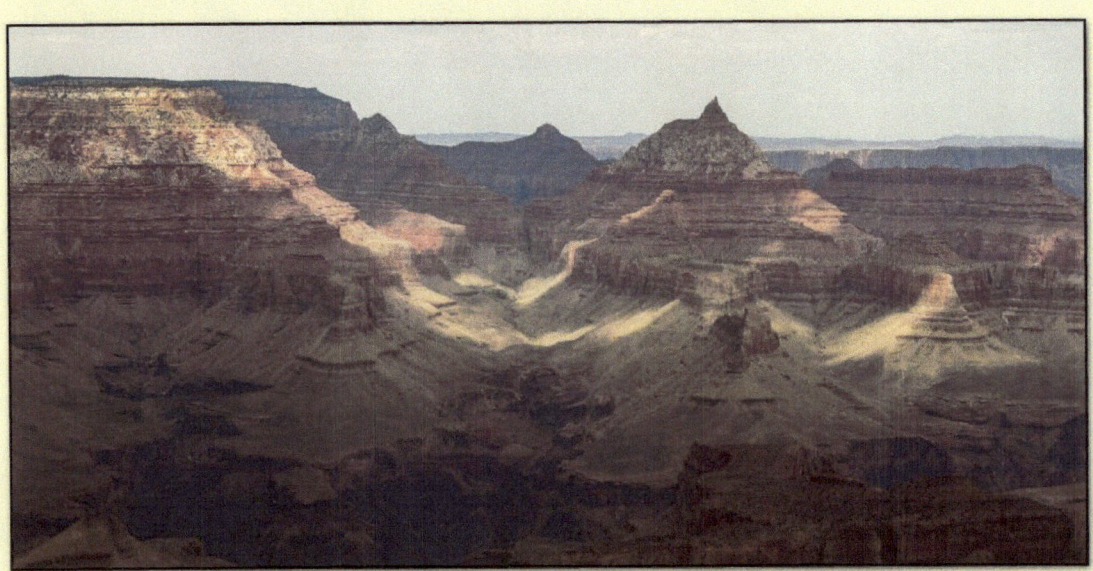

Adventures of the Kolb Brothers

Kolb studio is currently a popular spot for visitors of the Grand Canyon's south rim. The studio, which is also a lookout point for the canyon, is a place to remember the first men to photograph the beauty of the entire canyon.

The Kolb brothers began their adventure in 1902, venturing down to the bottom of the canyon in an effort to capture the beauty of the park.

Emery and Ellsworth Kolb are credited as two of the first men to capture the canyon through photography. They opened their own studio at the canyon to give them easy access to all of the area's great vistas.

Some of the most famous photos and film clips exploring this wonder were created by Emery and Ellsworth, which is why their names will live on for ages all over the Grand Canyon.

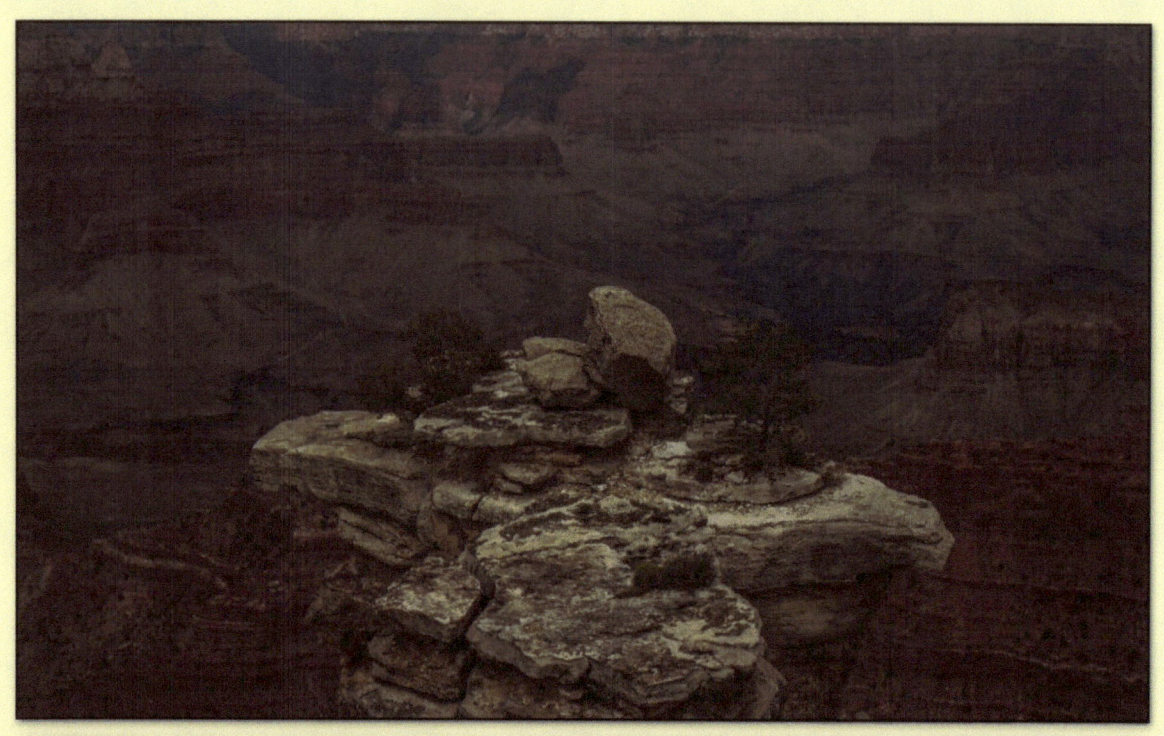
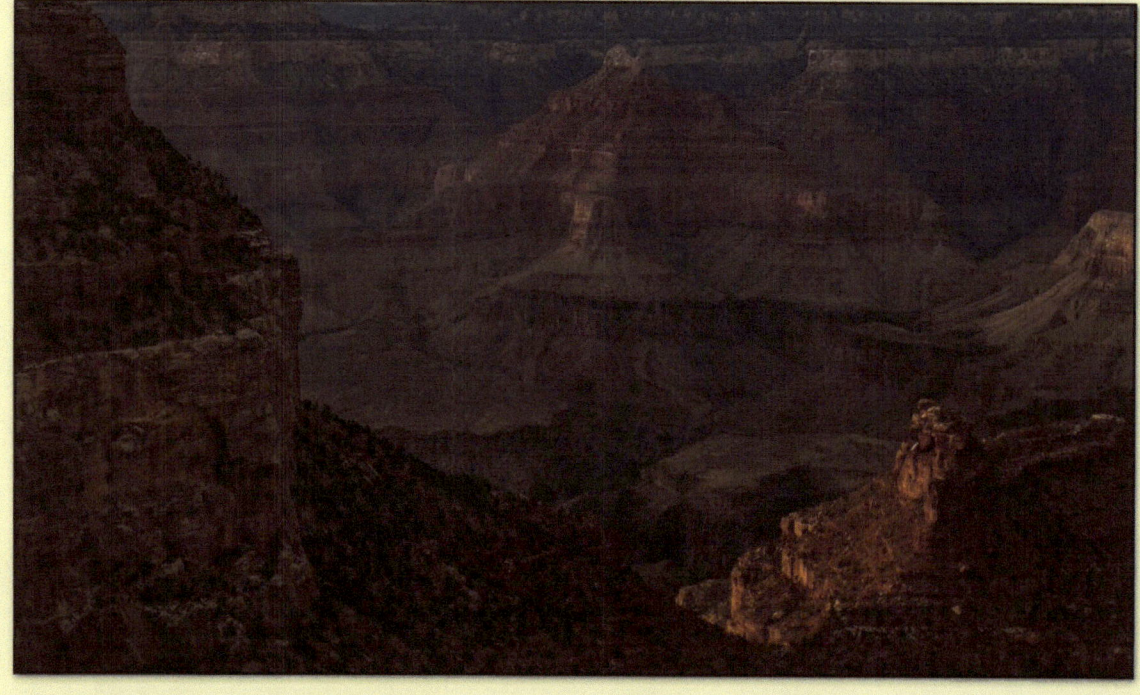

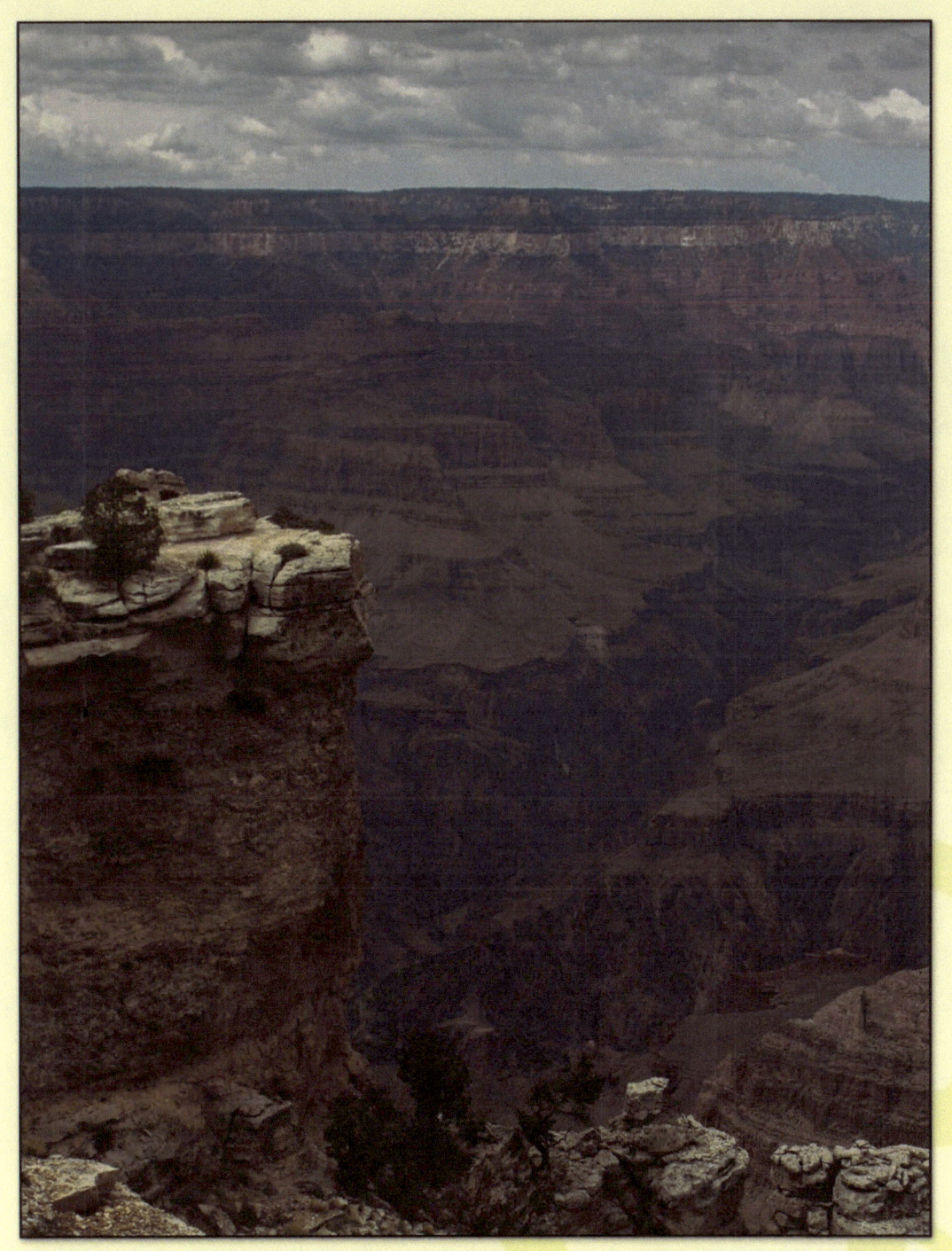

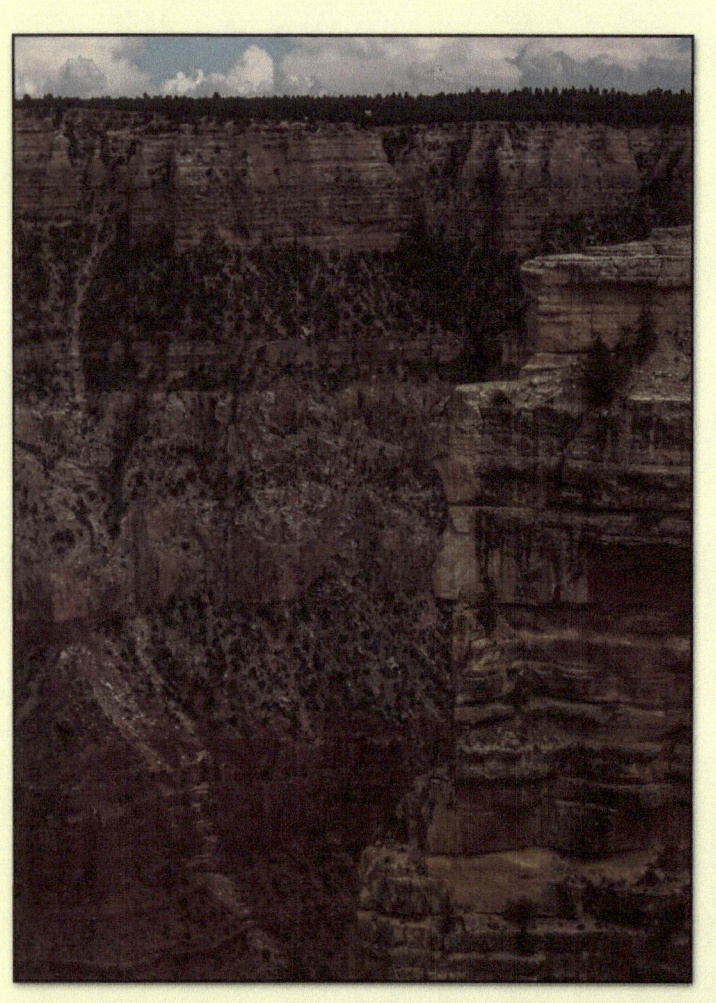
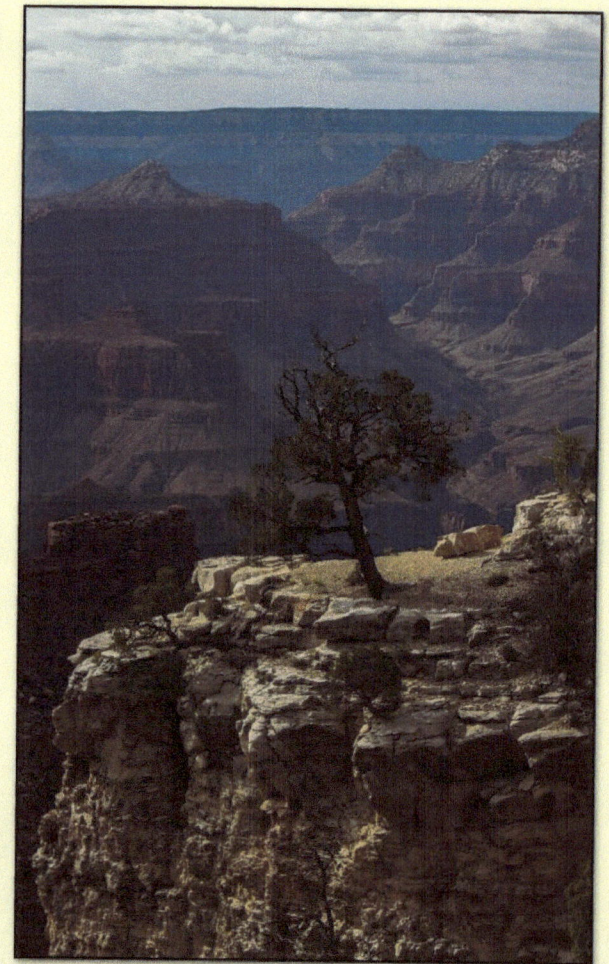

Desert View Drive

A long road that takes you passed a number of breathtaking views, Desert View Drive is the best way to leave or enter the park.

Marked lookouts along Desert View Drive include (in order from the entrance out) Desert View, Navajo Point, Lipan Point, Moran Point, Grandview Point, and Yaki Point. Although this route is typically less crowded than the other options, it is by far the most beautiful.

Other attractions along the way include the Watchtower, an old tower you can walk up, providing you with breathtaking views of the canyon, as well as the Tusayan Ruins and Museum.

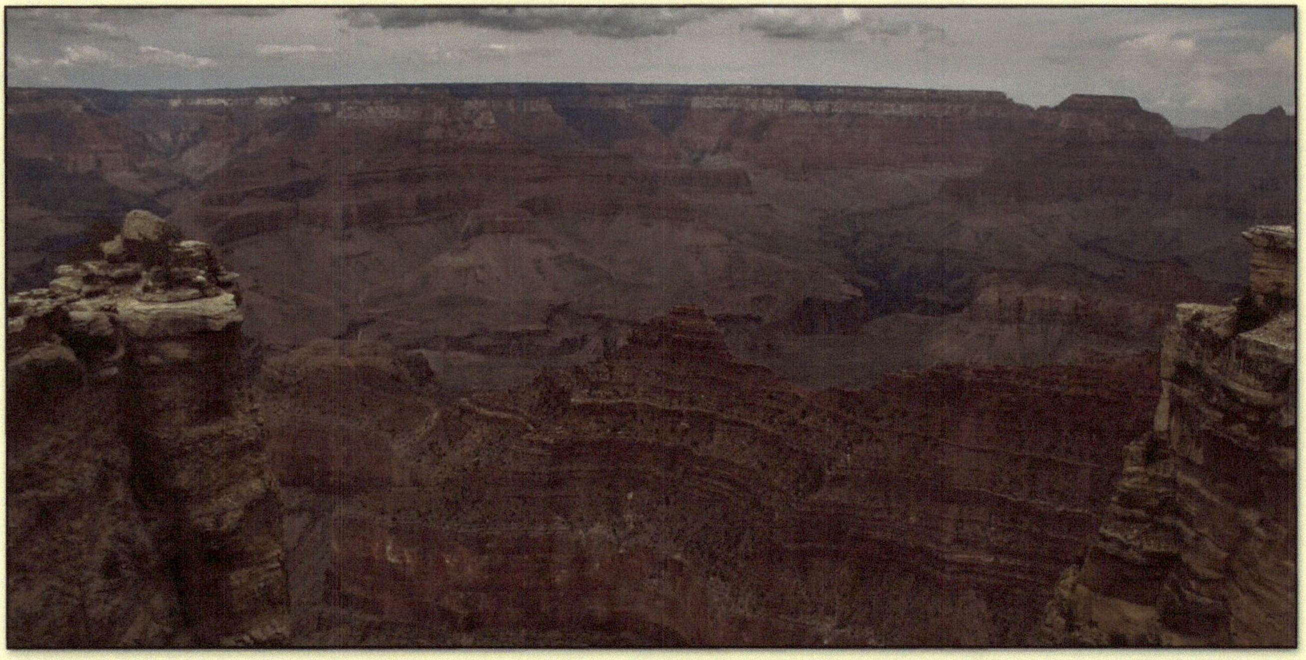

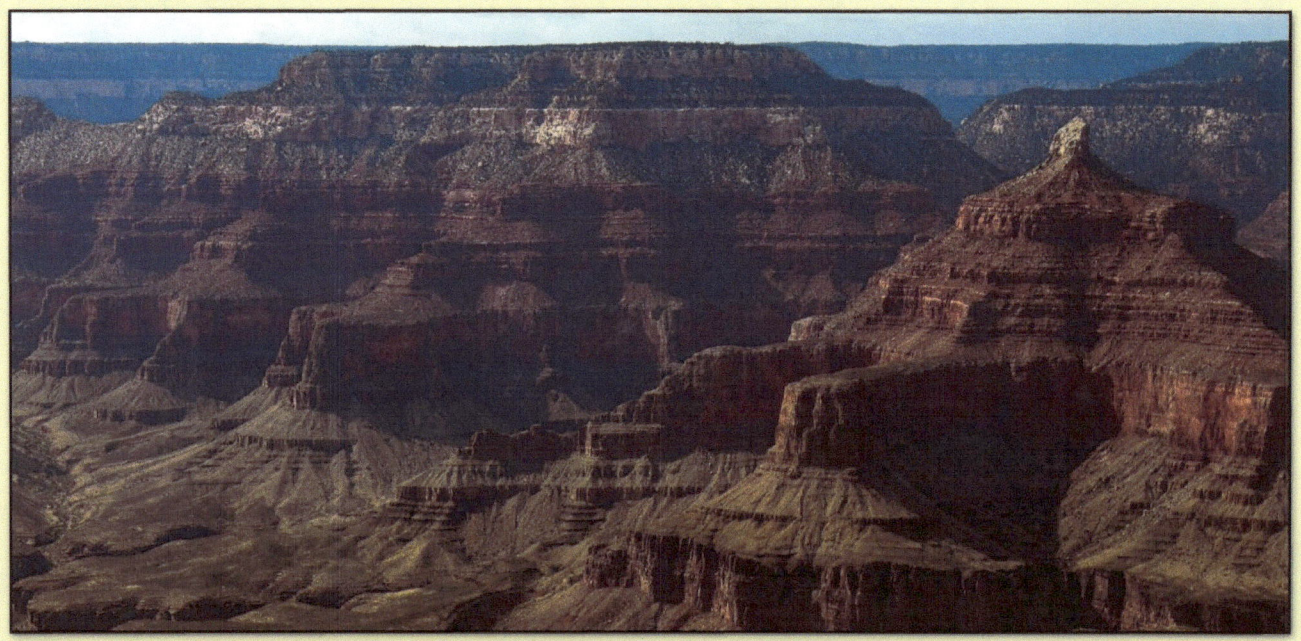

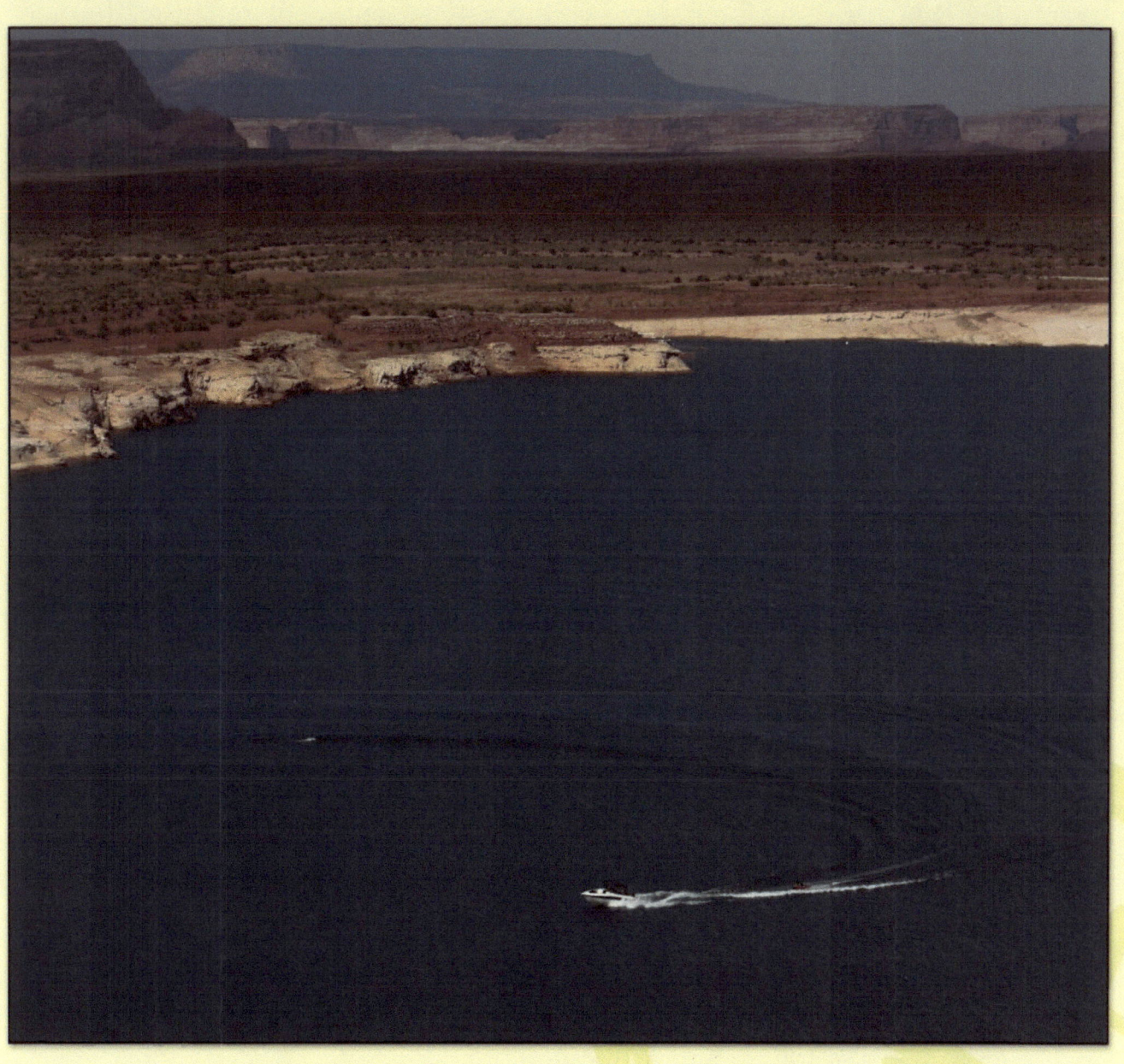

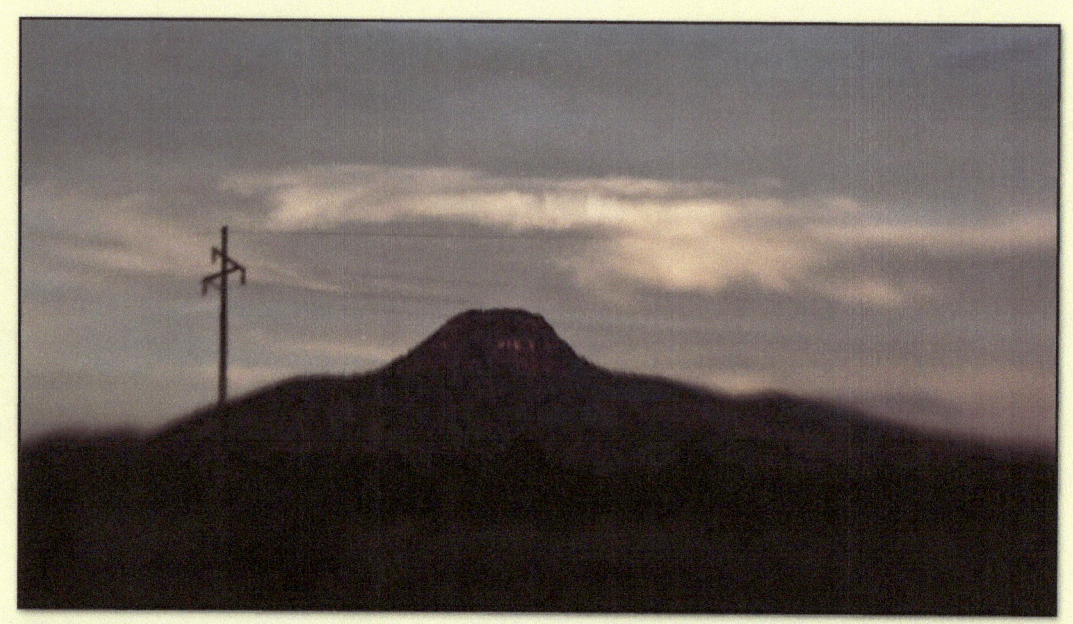

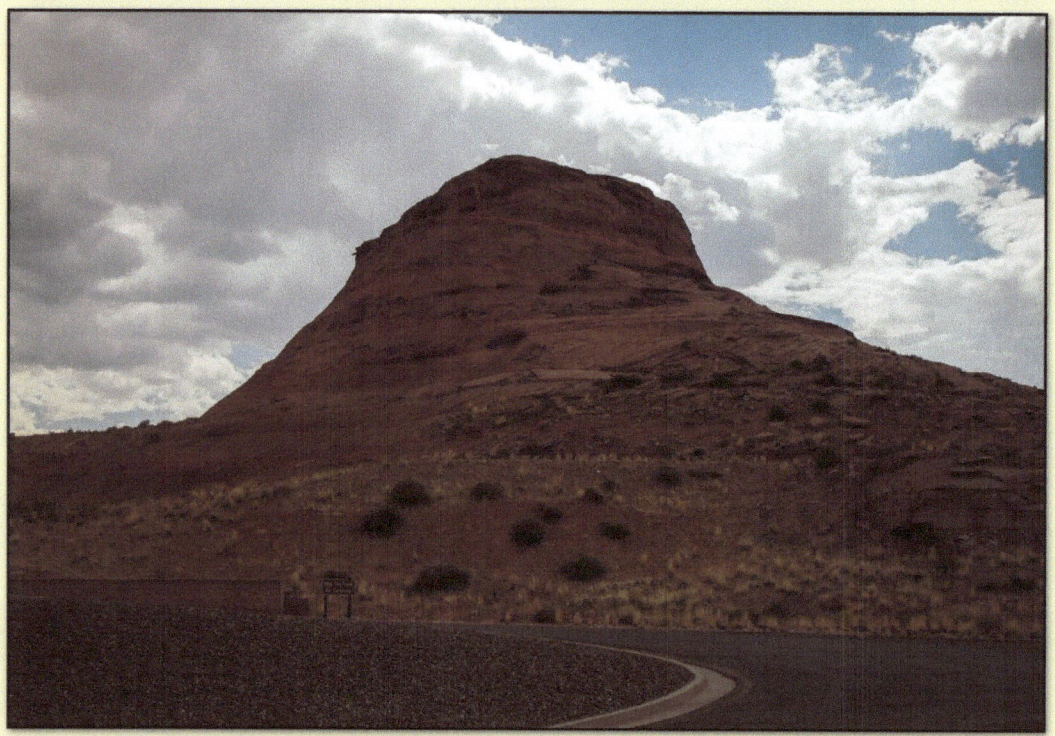

Outside of the Park - The Beauty of Red Rocks

Driving from Phoenix to Tusayan, right outside Grand Canyon National Park, one can take any route to get from point A to point B, but no drive beats the Red Rock Scenic Bypass.

A longer drive that is further in mileage and more out of the way than the other driving options, driving along the Red Rock Bypass takes you through the beautiful town of Sedona.

Popular sites to see in the area include Chapel Rock, Bell Rock, Sedona's famous vortexes, Verde Valley, Slide Rock State Park, as well as Red Rock State Park. Shopping and dining options are all lined up and down the main street of the town, featuring numerous art galleries.

This drive takes you on narrow, curvy roads, which can be difficult to navigate at night if you are not familiar with the area. Avoid driving this way too long after sunset, because when the sun goes down the roads get dark, fast.

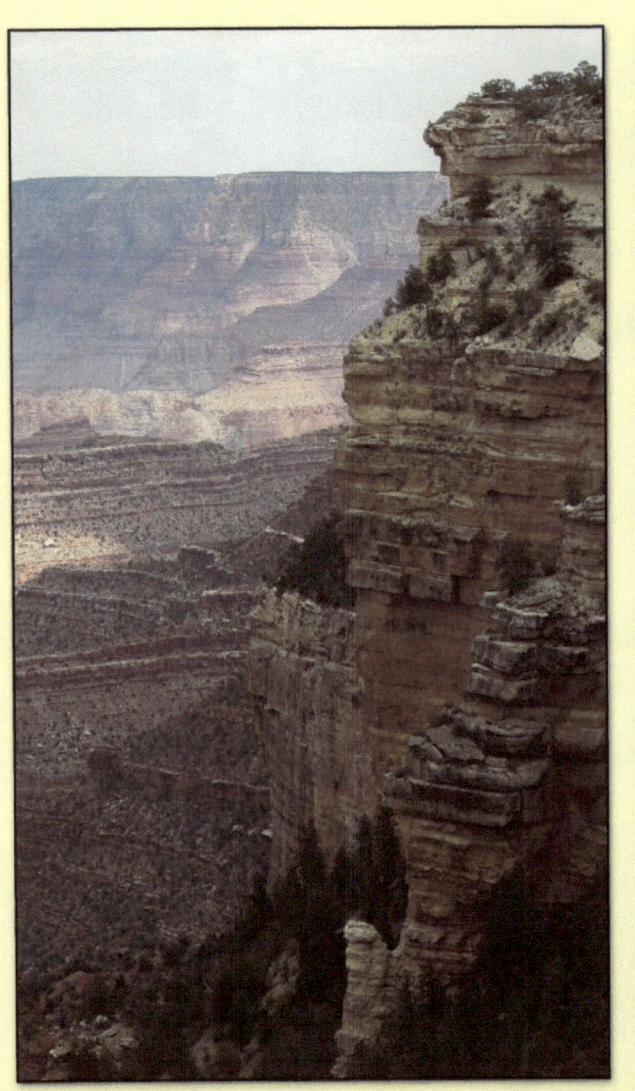
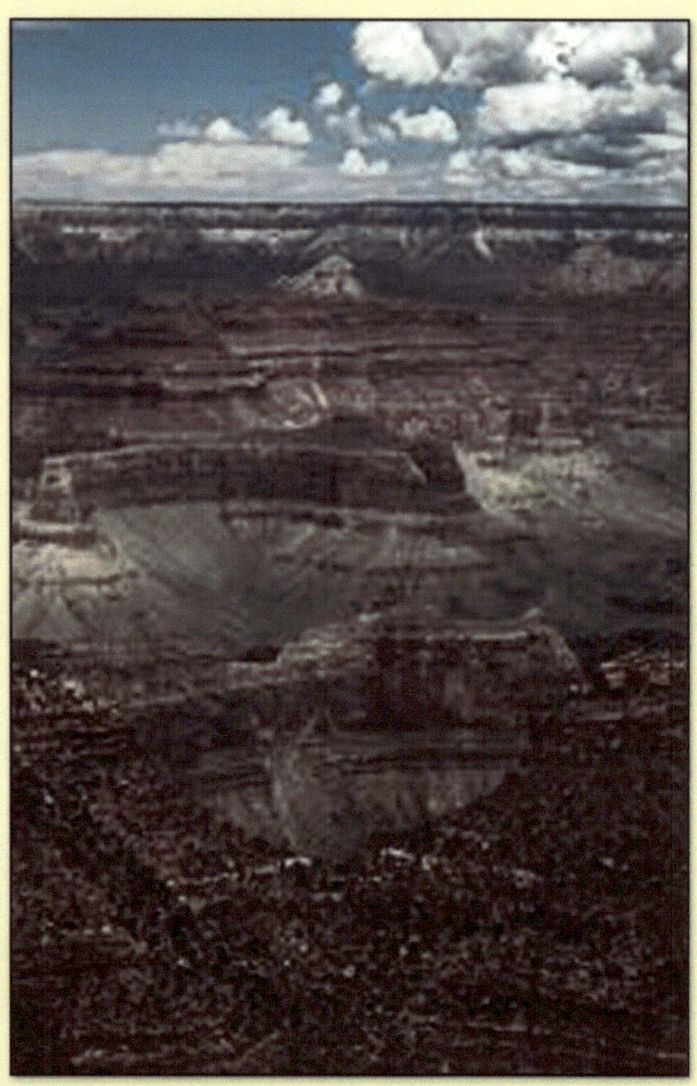

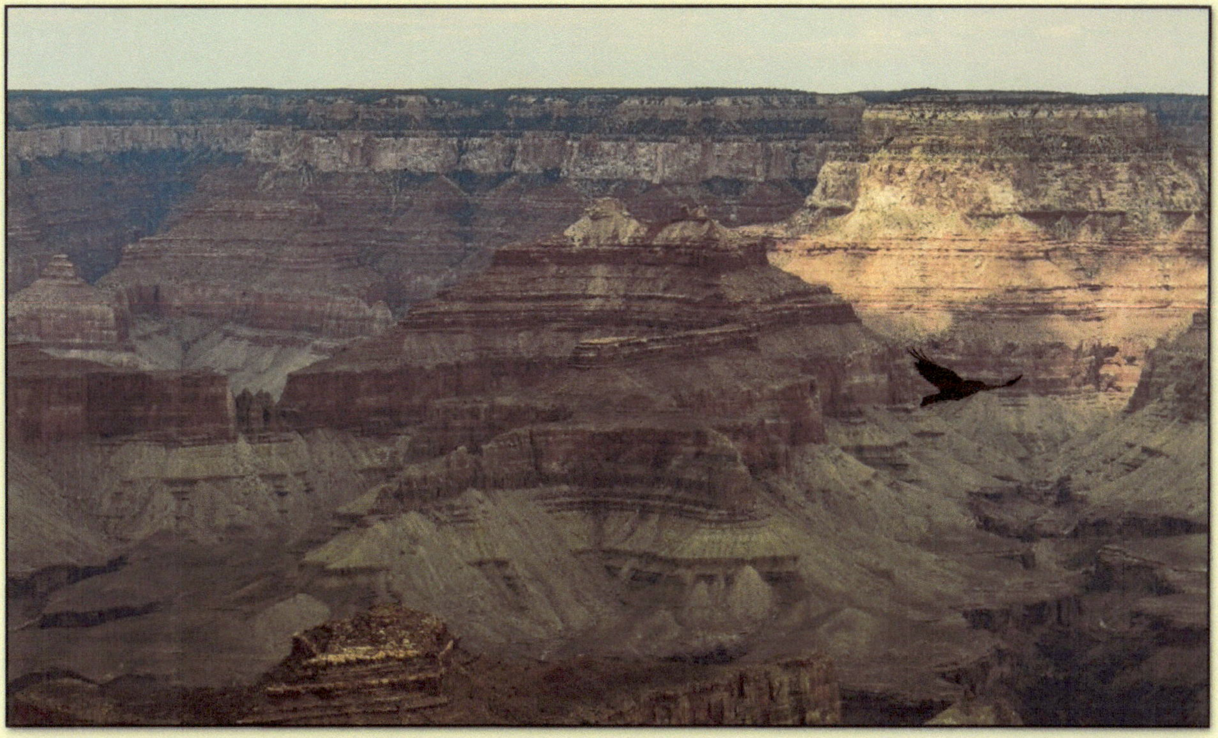

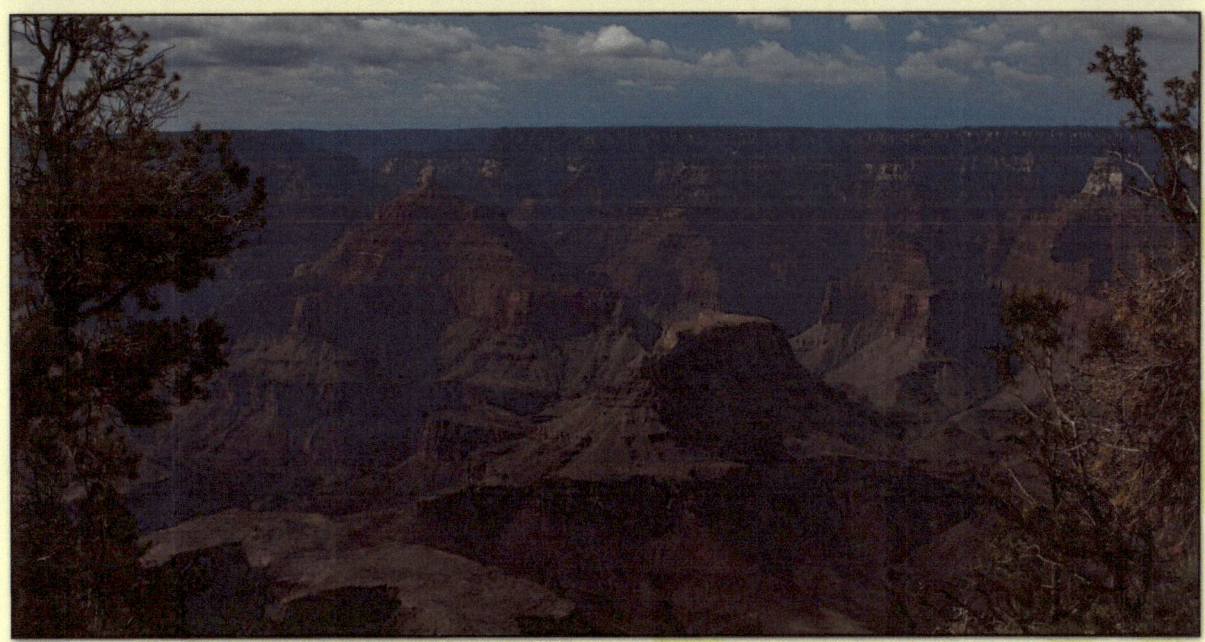

Historic Navajo Bridge at Grand Canyon National Park

The historic Navajo Bridge is an excellent place to take in all of the different views that the Grand Canyon offers.

The bridge is 750 feet in length and towers 470 feet above the Colorado River. If you are afraid of heights, this bridge may not be up your alley, but if you are an adventurer, the historic Navajo Bridge cannot be missed!

Near the bridge is a small visitors center where you can buy water and snacks, as well as authentic Navajo jewelry, home decor items and more.

More Activities to Do at the Grand Canyon

There is plenty to do at the Grand Canyon including:

South Rim mule rides

Hiking

Horseback riding

Helecopter rides through the canyon

Rafting down the Colorado River

Walk the Trail of Time

Climb the 70 foot watchtower at Desert View Point

Visit the Tusayan Museum

Visit the Yavapai Museum of Geology

Cross the Hualapai Skywalk

Check out the Shrine of Ages

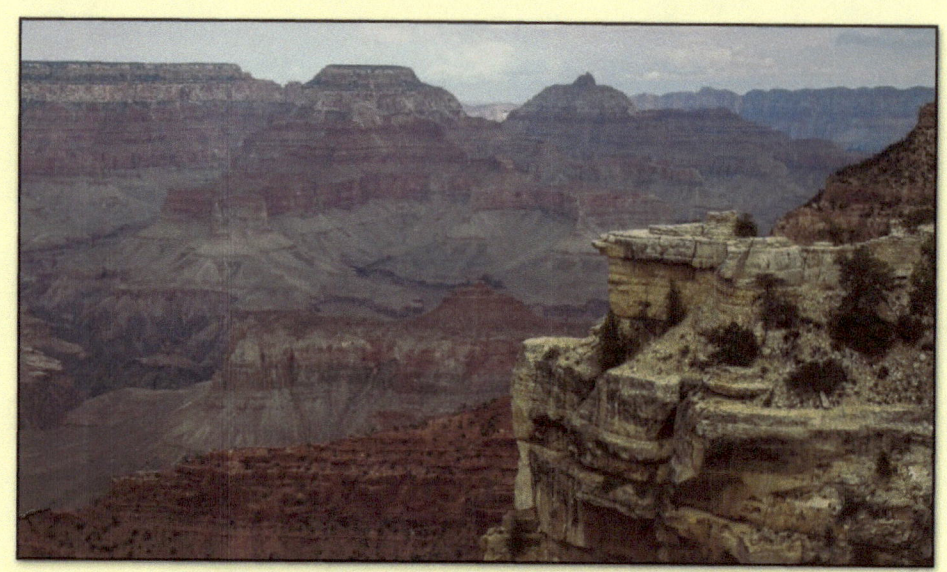

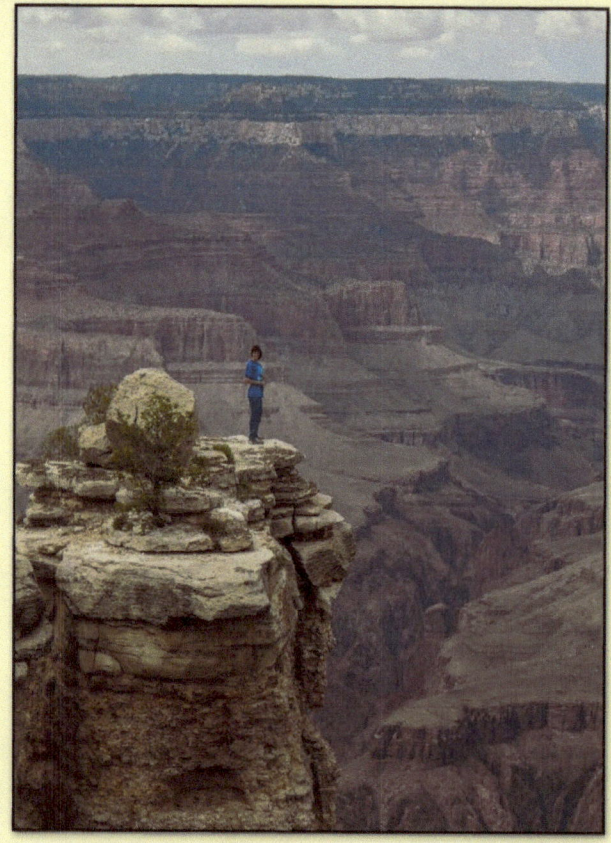

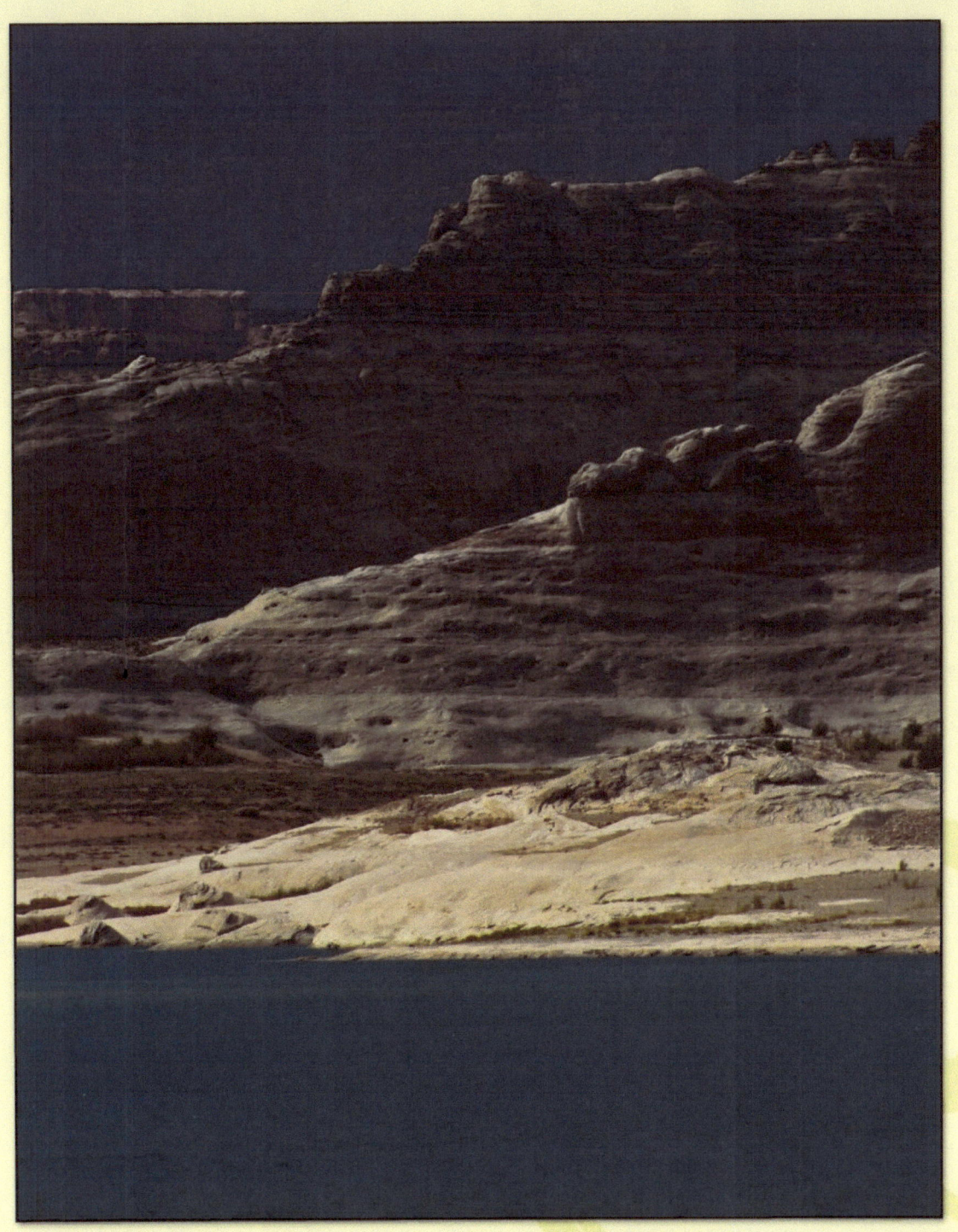

The Hidden Gems to Look for Near Grand Canyon National Park

The Chains- Located in Page, Arizona, The Chains is a swimming hole only accessible by hiking four miles round trip. The hike is well worth it however, as this spot is often deserted, making it scenic, relaxing and serene. If you choose to visit The Chains, be sure to bring plenty of water and sunscreen for the hike, as the heat in Page can get well into the 100s during the summer season.

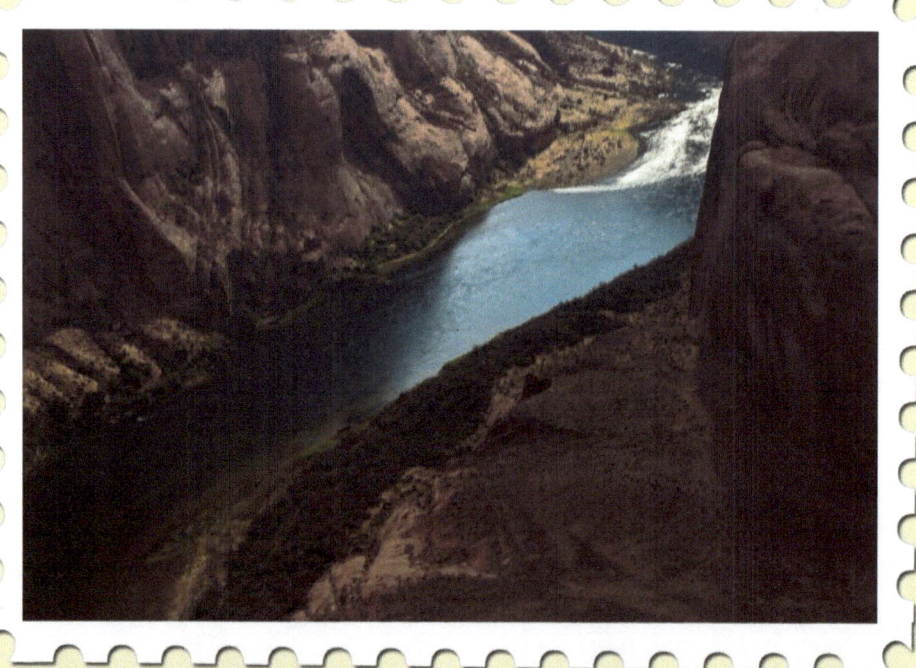

The Hanging Gardens- Just a few miles from The Chains you can find the Hanging Gardens, a Navajo Sandstone overhang covered in green plant life that juts right out of the beautiful red rocks. The Hanging Gardens is a half mile long trail that is easy to traverse due to the flat terrain.

Horseshoe Bend- Off the beaten path but well worth the drive, Horseshoe Bend is a scenic overlook located right off of US-89. Although the overlook is not easy to get to, requiring a short, yet extremely hot, uphill hike, the view is well worth the trek. Once you arrive at the edge of the cliffs, you will see the Colorado River in a horseshoe shape flowing around the canyon. Be sure to bring water with you, as the hike to the bend is not long, but very exhausting.

A Guide to the Grand Canyon's South Rim
by Kathleen Odenthal Romano

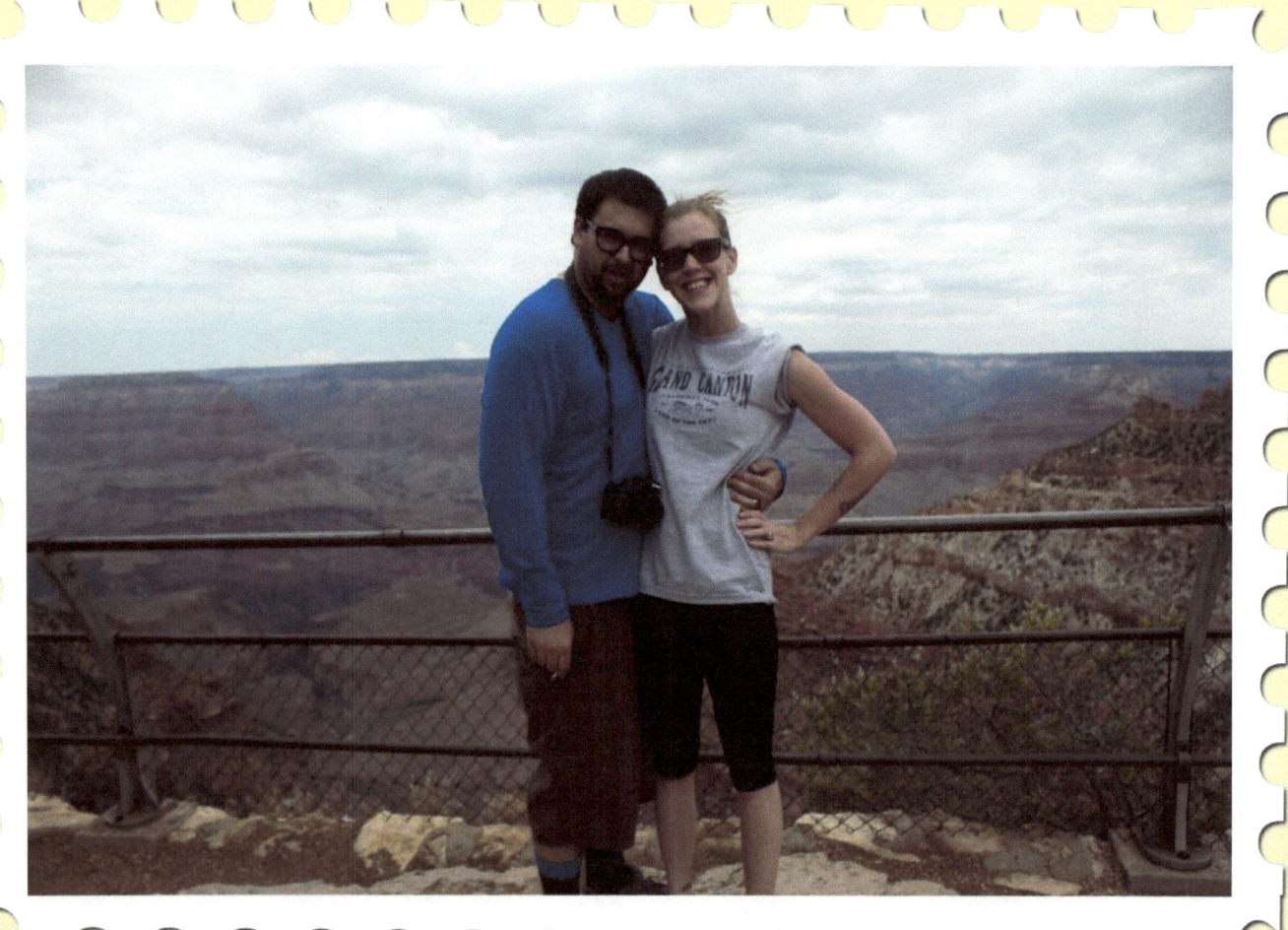

Thank you for reading Kathleen's guide to the Grand Canyon's south rim! If you enjoyed this book, be sure to check out her other photography books and travel guides available on Amazon.com.

Kathleen Odenthal Romano is a professional photographer and travel enthusiast. She loves to explore the world and document her adventures through photographs and share her experiences with others.

All images in this book are the sole ownership of the photographer (Kathleen Odenthal Romano). For permission to use any of the images, or to purchase a copy of one of the images, you can email Kathleen at kpmfineart@gmail.com or visit her on the web at kpmphotographyinc.com.